Sex Addiction
The Partner's Perspective

Sex and pornography addiction are growing problems that devastate the lives of partners as well as sufferers. *Sex Addiction: The Partner's Perspective* has been written to help partners and those who care about them to survive the shock of discovering their partner is a sex addict, and to help them make decisions about the future of their relationships and their lives. First and foremost it is a practical book, full of facts and self-help exercises to give partners a much-needed sense of stability and control. Like its sister book, *Understanding and Treating Sex Addiction*, it includes case examples and survey results revealing the reality of life for partners of sex addicts.

Sex Addiction: The Partner's Perspective is divided into three parts. **Part I** explores the myths surrounding sex addiction and provides up-to-date information about what sex addiction is and what causes it, before moving on to explain why the discovery hurts partners so much. **Part II** is about partners' needs and includes self-help exercises and strategies to help partners regain stability, rebuild self-esteem and consider their future. The controversial topic of co-dependency is also explored, with guidance on how to identify it, avoid it and overcome it. **Part III** focuses on the couple relationship, starting with the difficult decision of whether to stay or leave. Whatever the decision, partners will then find help and support for rebuilding trust and reclaiming their sexuality.

This book has been written to help partners not only survive, but grow stronger and move on with their lives, whether alone, or in a relationship. Readers will find revealing statistics and real-life stories shared by partners who kindly took part in the first UK survey of sex addiction partners. This book will be a valuable guide not only for partners, but also for the therapists who seek to support them on their journey of recovery.

Paula Hall is one of the UK's leading sex addiction specialists and the author of *Understanding and Treating Sex Addiction*. She created the Europe-wide Hall Recovery Course for people with sex addiction and the Hall Recovery Course for Partners. She is also a renowned speaker and trainer, and founder of the Institute for Sex Addiction Training.

Endorsement for Paula Hall's *The Partner's Perspective*

'I am grateful for the breadth and wealth of information found in Paula Hall's *The Partner's Perspective*! In an era when the term sex addiction is still confusing and misunderstood, loved ones of these "addicts" have been left wanting for understanding, support, and appropriate help. Partners of sex addicts have been isolated, misunderstood, and often without knowledgeable help or resources. Paula's new book is an excellent addition to available resources that address the trauma experienced by many partners in response to discovery of secret sexual behaviours in their loved ones. I believe this book will provide information, encouragement and hope to partners and relationships shattered by sex addiction, and become a valuable tool in partner recovery and healing!'

Barbara Steffens PhD, licensed professional clinical counselor; Certified clinical partner specialist, certified partner coach; Board certified coach, President, Association of Partners of Sex Addicts Trauma Specialists (APSATS)

'With *Sex Addiction: The Partner's Perspective*, Paula Hall has effectively shined a light on an otherwise much underserved clinical population: those spouses and partners traumatised and otherwise negatively hurt due to the ongoing sexual and/or emotional betrayal of a cheating spouse. Throughout the book, Paula recognises and elucidates how the emotional reactivity expressed by cheated-on partners at the height of their relationship-grief, is not necessarily indicative of co-dependency, or any other particular emotional disorder; but is in fact a natural and perfectly healthy response to the pain and distress of being habitually lied to, manipulated and ultimately betrayed. Ms Hall also acknowledges that the aftermath of endless cheating, affairs and even sexual addiction does not necessarily lead to the end of a relationship, as many couples grow beyond such damage to rebuild trust, and establish newfound intimacies. She makes clear that with useful professional guidance and hard work on the part of both partners, many such couples can regain trust and establish newly evolved intimacies and attachments.'

Robert Weiss LCSW, CSAT-S, US therapist, educator and author of 'Always Turned On': Understanding Sexual Addiction in the Digital Age

'Following the first UK survey of partners of sex addicts, Paula Hall highlights the extent of the distress and dilemmas of this considerable population. Challenging previous notions of theory about why partners choose to stay with addicts, she weaves an original and common-sense path. While acknowledging the value of some earlier thinking, she focuses on the trauma experienced by those whose world is not as they thought it was.

This is a long-awaited work for the UK. We now have an approach that reflects the diverse needs of those who find themselves with these challenges, offering shame reduction, hope and understanding. Where Paula Hall excels is in her breadth of therapy and counselling experience, as well as being a sex addiction specialist. The clear and accessible style, with many practical strategies for coping and moving forward, will be helpful for therapists and clients alike.'

Joy Rosendale MA Cert Ed, COSRT, CSAT 1 & 2 Partners' Programme Clinical Lead, Marylebone Centre London W1

Sex Addiction:
The Partner's Perspective

A comprehensive guide to understanding and surviving sex addiction for partners and those who want to help them

Paula Hall

Routledge
Taylor & Francis Group

LONDON AND NEW YORK

First published 2016
by Routledge
27 Church Road, Hove, East Sussex, BN3 2FA

And by Routledge
711 Third Avenue, New York, NY 10017

Routledge is an imprint of the Taylor & Francis Group, an informa business

© 2016 Paula Hall

The right of Paula Hall to be identified as author of this work has been
asserted by her in accordance with sections 77 and 78 of the Copyright,
Designs and Patents Act 1988.

British Library Cataloguing in Publication Data
A catalogue record for this book is available from the British Library

Library of Congress Cataloging in Publication Data
Hall, Paula.
   Sex addiction: the partners' perspective a comprehensive guide
   to understanding and surviving sex addiction for partners and
   those who want to help them/Paula Hall.
   pages cm
   Includes bibliographical references.
   1. Sex addiction. 2. Sex addiction – Treatment. 3. Man-woman
   relationships – Psychological aspects – Case studies. I. Title.
   RC560.S43H34 2016
   616.85′833 – dc23
   2015009433

ISBN: 978-1-138-77651-7 (hbk)
ISBN: 978-1-138-77652-4 (pbk)
ISBN: 978-1-315-76654-6 (ebk)

Typeset in Times New Roman
by Florence Production Ltd, Stoodleigh, Devon, UK

Contents

Introduction   1

PART I
Facing the reality of sex addiction   **3**

1 Does sex addiction really exist?   5

2 Understanding sex addiction   15

3 Why sex addiction hurts partners so much   29

PART II
Caring for partners' needs   **41**

4 Surviving the trauma of discovery   43

5 Understanding the cycle of reaction   59

6 Repairing self-identity and self-esteem   75

7 Facing the future   85

8 Identifying, avoiding and overcoming co-dependency   95

PART III
The couple relationship – make or break?   **107**

9 Can the relationship survive?   109

10 How sex addiction impacts couple relationships 117

11 Rebuilding trust 129

12 Reclaiming sex and sexuality 143

   Conclusion 155

   References 157
   Recommended reading and resources 161
   Index 165

Introduction

This book is long overdue and I'd like to start by apologising to all the partners, and professionals, who have patiently, and impatiently, waited for it. When I wrote *Understanding and treating sex addiction* 2 years ago, I had hoped to write a whole section for partners, but quickly discovered there was no room, and partners needed, and deserved, a book dedicated to them.

This book has taken many months to write, during which time I have worked with a growing number of partners, both individually and within groups, and have conducted a survey of 125 partners – all of whom have generously shared their experiences and their journey. I hope that, like me, you will learn from their wisdom and insight as you read through these pages.

The first lesson that I learned was that discovering your partner has sex or pornography addiction is traumatic, in a way that few have experienced and even less understand. Well-meaning friends and professionals may try to offer help and consolation, but it is often only through sharing with other partners that any sense of authentic identification can be found. Partners find themselves in free fall, as the world they previously knew is ripped from under them, and many fear they will never find solid ground again. Mindfulness guru John Kabett-Zinn said 'you can't stop the waves, but you can learn to surf' and it is my hope that, through this book, partners will learn how to keep their head above water and ride the destructive emotional waves that threaten to engulf their lives, and that therapists will become more proficient 'surf' instructors.

Part I focuses on the reality of sex addiction. Some people still doubt the existence of sex addiction and many who do accept it, do not understand it. The first three chapters are devoted to sharing information about what sex addiction is and why it hurts partners so much. Through these chapters I hope you will learn that sex addiction is not about sex, wanting too much or not being happy with what you have, but about a compulsive behaviour that meets deeper psychological needs and a condition that changes the structure of the brain, leaving rational decision-making and the genuine love and devotion to partners a distant memory.

In Part II the focus shifts specifically to the needs of partners and, using SURF as our acrostic, partners will learn how to Survive the trauma, Understand their reactions, Reclaim self-identity and Face the future. There is also a chapter exploring the controversial topic of co-dependency, which continues to confuse, damage and insult many already-traumatised partners.

Part III is about the couple relationship and starts with some food for thought for partners to digest as they consider the future of their relationship. The following chapters go on to explore in depth what is required to heal relationships broken by sex addiction, including how to improve communication, rebuild trust and reclaim sex and sexuality. You will also find information and guidance on the importance of 'therapeutic disclosure', which is an essential, but often under-utilised tool in partner recovery.

Much of this book has been written from a female, heterosexual perspective as this represents most of my clinical experience, but sex addiction affects male partners too, as well as gay and lesbian couples. There are more similarities than differences between these partner groups, but nonetheless I wish to acknowledge that some readers will rightly feel not enough has been said to address their individual needs.

I have also failed to escape using the pejorative label of 'addict', which those who have worked or trained with me know I desperately try to avoid. I do not believe that addiction should define a person, but rather it is a condition that people have. Hence I never refer to people with sex addiction as 'addicts', either when working directly with them or with their partners. But for the purpose of easy reading, I have relented, as referring to 'partner' and 'person with the addiction' became clumsy very quickly. Nonetheless, I maintain that the label of 'addict' is unhelpful for everyone.

Finally I would like to close by dedicating this book to all the partners who have so courageously shared their experience with me – those who have shared their traumatic experiences of personal betrayal and sorrow that so often go beyond words. Sex addiction is the most intimate wound that any partner can be forced to face, and the most brutal attack a relationship can be expected to endure. But partners do survive and so do many relationships, and it has been a profound privilege to work with the couples who have fought addiction together, as well as the partners who have taken the brave step to move on with life alone.

Part I

Facing the reality of sex addiction

'Face reality as it is, not as it was or as you wish it would be'
Jack Welsh

In these first three chapters we explore the reality of sex addiction. Many partners have never heard of sex addiction until it crashes into their lives and, understandably, most know little about it and some are sceptical that it really exists. In Chapter 1 we look at the arguments for and against the sex addiction label and the criteria establishing if someone is a 'sex addict'. Chapter 2 is devoted to understanding sex addiction from a biological, psychological and social perspective. We look at the different classifications of sex addiction, the most common causes and the essential treatment strategies. The chapter ends with an explanation of what 'recovery' means and looks like for people struggling with this condition. In Chapter 3 we see why sex addiction hurts partners so much and why the misconceptions of friends, family and misinformed helping professionals can inadvertently make the pain of discovery even worse.

1   Does sex addiction really exist?

Most partners do not discover their partner is a 'sex addict'. What they discover is that their partner has been unfaithful. More often than not, partners gradually drag out, or unravel, the painful reality that the person they most trusted in their life has betrayed them, not once, but repeatedly. The words 'sex addiction' may not enter the vocabulary for many weeks, months or even years after behaviours have been discovered. And when it is out there on the table, the first reaction of many partners is – really?

In the survey of 126 partners that was conducted to accompany this book, 30 per cent had heard of sex addiction before their partner's diagnosis, 25 per cent didn't believe it existed and 36 per cent thought it was just an excuse.

At the time of writing this book, sex addiction is still a controversial topic and, like many, you may be sceptical about the reality of the condition. In the survey, only 9 per cent believed sex addiction was a real problem when they first heard of their partner's problems, compared with nearly 79 per cent today. Thankfully, public and professional opinions are slowly beginning to change as issues of compulsive porn use become more and more prevalent and other explanations make less and less sense. But nonetheless, doubts and myths still prevail, and for partners of so-called 'sex addicts', those misunderstandings can have profound emotional effects. Because if sex addiction doesn't really exist, then what does that make their partners?

We have alternative words to sex addiction for people who have betrayed their partner multiple times; for those who have breached their partner's trust and deliberately acted in ways that they know would break their heart; for the men, and women, who seem to be incapable of fidelity, or those who choose to stay up late alone every night to watch porn. These words are mostly negative and abusive ones, though there are still significant gender differences. A man may get away with the euphemistic label of a 'player' or some might call him 'a typical bloke', or perhaps simply a 'bastard'. A woman may be called a 'nymphomaniac' or a 'sex kitten', or a 'bitch' and a 'slut'. If the behaviours are outside of what is deemed to be normal or commonplace, additional terms such as a 'freak', 'saddo' or even 'pervert' might be applied. All are value judgements about the character of the individual, character traits that are assumed to be the cause of the behaviour.

Sex addiction offers an alternative explanation to the character assassinations that are often thrown at people whose sexual behaviour crosses a partner's, or society's boundaries, but for some it is hard to accept. There are two main reasons for that which we will now explore.

Common objections to sex addiction

Sex addiction is just an excuse for moral failure

At the root of this common objection is the belief that if you're an 'addict' then you don't have to accept responsibility for the mistakes you've made in the past or the choices you make in the future. That is simply not true and, if it were, it would make treatment a waste of time and money. Addiction is not the opposite of choice. Someone with an addiction has still made choices about their behaviour, but those choices have been driven by something much deeper and more powerful than willpower. There is a difference between what motivates addictive behaviours and what motivates selfish, immoral behaviours – but in both cases, ultimately the individual does make a choice.

When someone has an addiction, their ability to choose is impacted by the biological and psychological components of their addiction – something we will look at in more depth in the next chapter. But for now it's important to understand that both the neurochemistry of addiction, and the unconscious psychological causes, can combine to make choice very difficult indeed. When you add the neurochemical dopamine (the common denominator in all addictions) to the reward-seeking engine of the brain, it's like rocket fuel; unresolved issues and unmet needs from childhood can render the breaking mechanism almost useless. Hence, when it comes to choice and addiction, it's like having the turbo-fuelled engine of a rocket, and the brakes of a bicycle.

However, when someone is able to recognise and resolve the damage to their braking system and learn practical ways of developing other fuels for their engine, then a far greater degree of choice can be enjoyed.

There's no doubt that some people do misuse the addiction label. 'It's not my fault I'm an addict', or 'he can't help it, he's addicted', but it's not true. While it is accurate to say that an addict is not responsible for whether or not they have an addiction, they are responsible for what they do with it once it has been identified. And taking that responsibility is essential to overcoming the behaviour.

The myth that addicts have no choice, or are powerless and have no control, is sometimes compounded by a lack of understanding of the 12-step groups that help so many millions of addiction sufferers. Step 1 encourages accepting powerlessness over addiction and Step 2 recommends handing over that power to someone or something else. On the surface this may sound like a cop-out, but the spirit of the steps is to help people reach out to others and get help and support in overcoming their addiction rather than trying to do it alone. In essence, the steps can be seen as empowering as they provide a strategy and community within which to reclaim control of one's life, rather than focusing on trying to control addiction.

Before we move on, it's worth thinking a little further about the notion of 'moral failure'. The questions around morality and sex addiction are commonplace and unique when compared with other addictions. As a society, we generally don't make anywhere near as many moral judgements about drinking too much as we do about someone who is deemed to have too much sex. We may look down our nose and worry about the binge-drinking youth, but mostly we assume that people will get over it and develop a healthy relationship with alcohol. And we generally have more compassion for those who develop alcohol dependency. But when it comes to sex it's quite a different matter. Sex has always been a popular topic for moralisers, not least because of the negative and limited views of most of the world's religions and there are some psychological professionals in the US (Klein 2012; Ley 2012) who openly object to the sex addiction label because they view it as something that pathologises what some would consider as 'normal' and 'commonplace' sexual behaviour. What is key to understand here is that it is not the type or amount of sexual behaviour that defines it as an addiction, but the dependency on it. Whatever your moral viewpoint, some people have lots of sex, some people don't. Some people believe in monogamy, some prefer open relationships. Some like lots of experimentation and sexual diversity, others are content with more familiar tastes. Sex addiction is not about sex, it's about addiction, as we will continue to explore.

You can't get addicted to sex

This is another very common objection to the sex addiction term and depending on how pedantic and scientific you want to be, there may be some truth to it. It has been widely accepted for many years that people can become addicted to chemicals such as drugs and alcohol – substances that cross the blood-brain barrier and alter the brain chemistry. What's known as 'behavioural' or 'process' addictions have also grown widely in acceptance (Hebebrand *et al.* 2014), but many still struggle with the word 'addiction' and choose instead, for example, to talk about pathological gambling or compulsive overeating. The reason for this is that there is not currently sufficient clinical evidence to prove that sex works in the brain in the same way as chemicals. We do know from brain scans that the same pathways that light up when someone uses cocaine also light up when we have sex. And there is recent evidence that the same areas of the brain are activated when porn addicts are triggered as when drug addicts are triggered (Voon *et al.* 2014). But these studies have not been replicated enough, nor has there been sufficient data collation of withdrawal symptoms and behaviour escalation to convince all the authorities. It is for these reasons, that 'sex addiction' and 'porn addiction' are not currently in what is known as the DSM (Diagnostic and Statistics Manual), which for many in the US is considered the final word on what is, and is not, a diagnosable condition.

Unlike some other mental health authorities, I choose to reserve judgement on whether or not the term 'sex addiction' is scientifically accurate, as the field of addiction is changing so fast as our ability to research and understand the human brain expands. In the field of addiction, the impact of attachment and trauma on the brain, as well as the psychological impacts, are increasingly being recognised as significant contributing factors (Fisher 2007; Flores 2004) and our understanding of craving, satiation, tolerance and escalation are also changing as we learn more about the neurochemistry of the brain. These findings are also affecting our understanding of compulsive overeating, which is increasingly being recognised as a type of addiction (Fortuna 2012; Hebebrand *et al.* 2014). As with sex, there are undoubtedly some people who simply overeat out of greed but, according to *Frontiers in psychiatry* (Meule 2011), food addiction is an increasing reality.

The American Association for Addiction Medicine (ASAM) has adopted a new definition of addiction in line with the latest brain studies, stating that 'Addiction is a primary, chronic disease of brain reward, motivation, memory and related circuitry'. The DSM has also changed its listing of addiction in the latest edition, to a single category heading of 'addictive disorders' under which are the subheadings of 'alcohol use disorder', 'substance use disorder' and 'gambling disorder', with 'internet use disorder' being listed as warranting further research. What is common to both is that the emphasis has shifted from the substance or process to the physical and psychological symptoms of addiction.

While research continues to determine whether or not sex and pornography can become 'addictive' in the same way as other substances and behaviours, perhaps what is most important is to decide whether or not the accuracy of the term 'addiction' really matters to you or not. While the professionals decide what to call it, it undoubtedly continues to be a growing problem. For partners, the pain is probably the same whatever you call it, but the routes to overcoming it – for both you and your partner – may be very different. It is time for an example.

Jenny

Jenny did not believe that sex addiction existed. She had worked for many years in a hostel for homeless men with alcohol and drug issues and her husband did not look, or behave, even faintly like her wards. They were a middle-class, respectable family; her husband had a good job as a teacher and was a good father to their two small children. Ten months ago she found a message string on his phone from another woman saying she was 'looking forward to meeting him'. She questioned him immediately as she scrolled through other messages on his phone before he had chance to snatch it back. That's when she found the pictures, as well as sexually graphic texts from a further six women. John crumbled and confessed to a long-standing porn problem that had recently escalated to visiting masseurs. It was six months later that I met them both, and having done some research, John was convinced he had a sex addiction and was desperate for help to get back on track as well as save his marriage. But Jenny said it was too late. She had accompanied him to the meeting to see if I could convince her that the condition existed, but she could not believe that an upstanding man such as John could behave like that, unless he was simply a low-life fraud like her father who had apparently abandoned her mother when she was five. Like all of us, Jenny had her own story that influenced her response, and her choice was to blame John – not an addiction.

Before we move on, there is a further issue that is often raised which causes confusion.

But my partner's behaviour isn't really about sex

Partners of people with compulsive pornography problems often wonder if the sex addiction label can be accurate for them. Similarly there are an increasing number of people getting hooked on the adult hook-up sites, creating and checking profiles on a regular basis and chatting to potential partners. But they never meet – they have never actually had sex with any of them. Of course, for a partner, that is still a significant breach of trust and hence can cause a lot of pain, but is it the same as sex addiction? As said previously, sex addiction isn't about sex, it's about addiction.

There are many, many different behaviours that someone with sex addiction can engage in, for some it's all online, such as pornography, chat rooms, web-cam sex, while for others it is also offline, such as visiting sex workers, multiple affairs or cruising. What defines addiction is the dependency on something as a mood regulator, the exact nature of that substance or behaviour is not relevant to the definition. In other words, if you are an alcoholic, it's the alcohol you become dependent on, whether it's gin or whisky, beer or tequila is irrelevant. Similarly, in sex addiction it is the dopamine hit of the 'buzz' that the person becomes dependent on, not the actual type of behaviour. Tastes may develop, as they do with alcohol drinkers and some will have their preferences, but as the addiction escalates, so does the repertoire of behaviours. For many people with sex addiction, hunting for the perfect image or video clip, or spending hours on 'the chase' is as big a part of the addiction as the orgasm, if indeed they have one. Sex addiction is not about fulfilling a sexual need, in the same way that chronic overeating is not about fulfilling hunger. Hence, the sexual activity is not really relevant.

The evidence for sex addiction

Perhaps the biggest indicator of whether or not a condition really exists is the number of people who come forward for help.

Deirdre Sanders, the agony aunt of *The Sun* newspaper said:

> Sex/porn compulsion/addiction hardly existed among the hundreds of problems readers sent in to me each week at the start of the century, but now never a day goes by without me hearing from readers troubled by their or their partner's habit, going through all the age ranges, from scarcely into their teens to pensioners (personal communication).

Relate centres up and down the country are rapidly developing their services to addicts, partners and couples to cope with the demand, and I am training an ever-growing number of professionals every year from a variety of therapeutic communities to help them meet the needs of their clients. Many professionals would agree that porn addiction is reaching epidemic proportions. Online peer support groups for young guys trying to give up porn have unenviable numbers, reaching into hundreds of thousands.

In addition, there are a growing number of scientists and clinical and social researchers collating data to try to determine biological, psychological and causational facts, as well as a host of sociopolitical experts who are exploring the realities of sex and porn addiction in order to develop appropriate educational and preventative materials and methods.

If you're asking yourself 'if sex was really addictive, wouldn't we have known about it long, long ago?' or 'how come we're only just hearing about this condition now?'. Well, the answer, at least in part, is that as we've become a more sexually liberated society we're able to talk about the darker side more openly, and also access it. But the most significant reason for the stratospheric explosion in sex and porn addiction is the internet. There is now more opportunity to be a sex addict than at any other time in history. And while there is still minimal education about the potential risks of addiction, more and more people are getting caught in the snare. Many of those who may have had a low-level problem pre-broadband have found that the advent of limitless free pornography and endless adverts for other adult services has catapulted them into severe addiction. With the advent of the smartphone and still-limited success of blockers and filters, who knows where we'll be in 10 years' time? It is my sincere hope that, as a society, we will quickly accept the reality of sex addiction and work together to not just treat it, but prevent it.

Is my partner a sex addict?

Having established that sex addiction is a real problem, it's now time to confirm if this is what your partner is struggling with. If he/she hasn't already seen a professional for an assessment, or completed any other kind of online or written self-assessment tool, then I would recommend that they answer the questions below that I use in the first stage of my assessment process.

If you answer yes to five or more of the following questions then you may be struggling with sex addiction and would benefit from making an appointment for a full assessment.

1 Does your sexual behaviour have a negative impact on other areas of your life such as relationships, work, finances, health, and professional status?
2 Does your sexual behaviour contradict your personal values and potentially limit your goals in life?
3 Have you tried to limit your sexual behaviour or stop it altogether, but failed?
4 Are you more tempted to engage in sexual behaviour when you're experiencing difficult feelings such as stress, anxiety, anger, depression or sadness?
5 Are you secretive about your sexual behaviours and fearful of being discovered?
6 Do you feel dependent on your sexual behaviour and struggle to feel fulfilled with any alternative?
7 Have you noticed that you need more and more stimuli or risk in order to achieve the same level of arousal and excitement?
8 Do you find yourself struggling to concentrate on other areas of your life because of thoughts and feelings about your sexual behaviour?

9   Have you ever thought that there might be more you could do with your life if you weren't so driven by your sexual pursuits?

10   Do you feel as if your sexual behaviour is out of your control?

11   Do you currently, or have you in the past, struggled with any other addictions, compulsive behaviours or eating disorders, such as drug or alcohol addiction, compulsive gambling, gaming, work or exercise, or collecting?

12   Has anyone in your family currently, or in the past, struggled with any addictions, compulsive behaviours or eating disorders such as those listed above?

For some people, this questionnaire is sufficient to give a pretty good idea of whether the sex addiction label fits, but if you find that your partner is perhaps borderline, or if you're still not convinced that the behaviours are compulsive, rather than chosen, then the following question might help further.

Is this behaviour out of character for your partner?

In other words, in every other area of your life and relationship together, would you normally describe your partner as loving, open, honest, caring, trustworthy and reliable? Has this behaviour, or the extent of the behaviour, shocked you to the core? Would your friends and family, the people who know you and love you most, find it hard to believe what your partner has done? If your answer to this question is a resounding 'yes' then your partner is most likely to be suffering from sex addiction. That is perhaps the most plausible explanation. The harsh reality of addiction is that it leads good people to do bad things. If your answer to this is 'no', he/she has always kept secrets from me and we have often argued about appropriate behaviours and boundaries, then you may have bought this book in vain.

Jan

Jan was convinced that her husband Geoff was a sex addict. Like many partners, she stumbled upon a history of infidelities, dating back to most of their marriage. He was adamant that he was not addicted and that he would have no problem stopping his behaviour if he wanted to. He answered 'yes' to just two questions – numbers 1 and 6 – and they were only a yes because he knew that Jan would be devastated if she found out, something he had tried very hard to prevent. Geoff described himself as a traditional 'ladies' man'. He had the kind of job that allowed him the freedom to meet lots of women and an innate charm and good looks that made seduction easy. He had always kept his private life 'private', never talking to Jan about his friends, his work, or his finances or anything that he felt was 'none of her business'. They had argued about this for years, along with what Jan described as his blatant flirting with other women, which she felt was deeply disrespectful. Jan wanted Geoff to be a sex addict, because then perhaps he would change. Reluctantly she came to realise he was not; he was nothing more than a philanderer, and perhaps that could not be treated.

To conclude, there are many advantages to the label 'sex addiction', both for partners and for the person with the problem. In the survey, 62 per cent found the label 'very or extremely helpful', 23 per cent felt neutral about it and 15 per cent didn't find it helpful. If your partner is a sex addict then there is help for you and help for them. If this problem is an addiction, then you can rest assured that it is no reflection on you or on your relationship. In the same way that no one would blame a partner for alcoholism, there is no reason to feel any blame or self-doubt if your partner has sex addiction. Perhaps most importantly, if you still love your partner and he or she is willing to get into recovery, and if you both want the relationship to work, then it is possible. It is hard work for some, and for most it takes time, but nonetheless, it can be done.

2 Understanding sex addiction

The term 'sex addiction' describes any pattern of out-of-control sexual behaviour that causes problems in someone's life. It is not the type of behaviour that defines addiction, but the dependency on the behaviour and the inability to stop in spite of negative consequences.

To understand any kind of addiction, you need to recognise that it is much, much more than a bad habit that has been developed over a period of time. Addiction has a function, a psychological purpose (Dodes 2002). Sex addiction is a strategy used to alleviate negative emotions and create positive ones. But addictions are more than purely psychological, they are also biological.

Pleasure is a physical process triggered by chemicals in the brain, primarily dopamine, endorphines and adrenalin. These chemicals are all naturally occurring, and someone with a chemical addiction heightens the impact of these chemicals by introducing others, whereas a sex addict has developed a super-fast highway in their brain to reach them faster. Primarily, addiction is fuelled by the chemical dopamine. It is a chemical that makes us want and seek out reward, but not a chemical that alone gives us pleasure. Hence some addicts find themselves getting hooked on activities that they don't even enjoy (Doidge 2008).

The brain is made up of literally millions of neural pathways that carry the necessary messages that make us think, feel and act, and there are a specific set of pathways responsible for delivering the feelings of pleasure. If we always access those pathways in the same way, they will become stronger, and other pathways that might have previously been used to access the pleasure chemicals become weaker. This is the principle of learning – the more we do something, the better we get at it. But in addiction, while those pathways become more fixed, they also become less effective at delivering the desired effect, which is why addicts find they need more stimulation in order to get the same effect (Blum *et al.* 2000; Duvauchelle *et al.* 2000). This is what is known within the addiction field as tolerance and escalation. You may have experienced something similar if you always have the same alcoholic drink, or when a favourite sugary snack loses its appeal.

As well as changes in the reward pathways, people with addiction often experience difficulties with impulse control, deferring gratification and making judgements about harmful consequences – all processes that involve the frontal cortex of the brain and underlying white matter. These areas of the brain are altered by addiction and, since they are still maturing in adolescence, this is why early exposure is believed to be a significant factor in the development of addiction.

Recently it has also been highlighted that the internet can impact our brain chemistry (Hudson-Allez 2009). It seems that when we are looking at the fast-moving images of the internet we tap into a different part of the brain. That feeling of losing touch with time and space that many of us can experience as we waste hours on eBay or research an interesting holiday destination is not purely psychological, it's the impact the internet has on the orientation of our brain. Hence when someone with sex addiction uses the internet it seems that the pleasure pathways are amplified and accelerated.

Internet pornography can be especially easy to get hooked on because of the way it works on the brain, being a 'supernormal stimuli'. A supernormal stimuli is the term used when we find our biological drives and instincts override our common sense, such as when we gorge ourselves on beautiful cupcakes or, for the addict, lose hours looking at porn. Our brains naturally seek novelty, and the drive for both food and sex are essential survival strategies. Internet pornography provides endless opportunities for novelty and reward and it is suggested that it is the perfect laboratory for witnessing neuroplastic changes (Hilton 2013).

Addiction is a disease of the brain that disrupts the circuitry of the brain and challenges control. Continued chemical misuse or behavioural acting out changes the chemistry of the brain, and the brain literally becomes dependent on the chosen drug or activity to feel pleasure and reduce pain. But brains can change back. They can be rewired again.

When sex addiction starts

The vast majority of people with sex addiction say their problem started before the age of 16 (40 per cent) and, for some (6 per cent), under the age of 10 (www.sexaddictionhelp.co.uk 2014). The seeds of sex addiction have almost always been sown and, for many, will already have taken root long before the relationship began. That is important for partners to know because it can help to prove the point that the addiction is no reflection on the relationship. A good relationship can make addiction become dormant for a while, but it won't cure it, which means that, regrettably, it is always only a matter of time before the addiction starts again.

Before we go on to look at the different types of sex addiction and how it starts, it's important to understand that what follows are 'explanations' not 'excuses'. One of the challenges of working with partners is that exploring the root cause can sometimes feel like a cop-out, and many partners will rightly say, 'that doesn't make it OK' or 'he/she may have had a difficult childhood, but they're adult now and they still chose to betray me'. Another common observation is that many people experience childhood difficulties but don't become an addict, so why did my partner?

Regrettably there is no single or simple answer to why anybody develops sex addiction. Understanding how something came to be, whether that's how someone became an addict or how you chose the relationship you're in or the job that you do, is almost always a complex interweaving of many different factors, many of which are dependent on another.

For example, if you're an acclaimed violinist, the chances are that your love of music started in early childhood, and from an early age you learned that you had an innate musical talent. Perhaps your parents encouraged you to listen to and play music and your passion was nurtured and your efforts and accomplishments praised. Negative events may have played a role too. Perhaps your first violin was inherited from your late grandfather who you miss very much, but who inspired you to commit to the instrument. If you also had the financial resources to pay for lessons and perhaps go and see live concerts to feed your ambition, and your local secondary school happened to be known for its excellent music teaching, then your journey to success had an excellent start. However, changing just a few key factors or introducing a discriminating wild card such as illness or parental separation might have changed your direction and set you on a very different path. Understanding the fragility of a life path is important because it can help us to understand why people with an almost identical history might develop very differently. It can also help us not to place undue blame or regret on one single incident or circumstance, something that is especially important in sex addiction where shame can play such a crucial role.

When looking at the causes of sex addiction, it is important to ask two questions. The first is, 'why does someone become an addict?' and the second, 'why did they become addicted to sex'. The answers to the first question generally reside in childhood whereas the answers to the second, usually around the time of puberty and adolescence.

Classifications of sex addiction

Although there are a significant number of characteristics common to everyone who develops sex addiction, there are differences in the extent

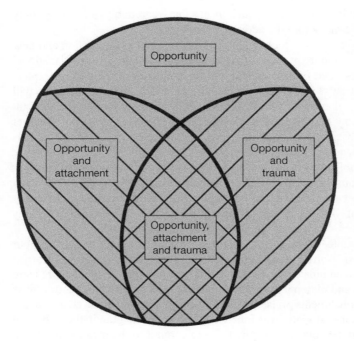

Figure 2.1 The OAT model

of the addiction and style. Broadly speaking, addiction is trauma-induced, attachment-induced or opportunity-induced or, in some cases, a combination of two or three (Hall 2013).

As you can see from Figure 2.1, opportunity is present in each of the three classifications of addiction, but, in addition, some people also have difficulties with attachment and/or trauma. Some years ago it was believed that all addiction had its roots in either attachment or trauma, but as pornography has become increasingly prevalent, so have the people who stumble into sex addiction with no prior difficulties.

We will briefly look at each of the types and how they can get set up in childhood and adolescence, but if you would like to read up in more detail on sex addiction, do get a copy of *Understanding and treating sex addiction*, which focuses specifically on the person with the addiction.

Opportunity-induced addiction

Whatever a person's history and individual circumstances, if there was no opportunity they wouldn't 'act out'. The reality of the Western world today is that 'opportunity' is everywhere. However, some people's brains are more predisposed to take that opportunity if they have a history of addiction (Hall 2013). As we will see later in this chapter, if people have a history of trauma or of attachment difficulties, they are also more likely to get hooked. Sex is now available anywhere and everywhere – online and offline. Whether you're male, female, queer, straight, gay, bi or anywhere else on a spectrum, you can find anything you desire easily and anonymously. Indeed, you can find a whole load of stuff you don't desire, but get hooked nonetheless. No addiction can exist without opportunity and, in the absence of adequate education and advice, people will experiment and explore and take risks that they didn't know were there. It is the nature of adolescence, when most addictions start, that we like new and pleasurable experiences, and which ones we choose to follow and for how long is dependent on our life experiences. We will go on to explore these in a moment, but it is important to highlight that society is responsible for some of the causes of sexual addiction, in particular, our policies on internet pornography and sex education. I am not trying to suggest that we should enforce some kind of sexual prohibition, but in the same way that we teach and encourage healthy eating and responsible drinking, so we should establish appropriate public information for healthy sexuality – information that allows people to make informed choices rather than blindly stumbling into addiction as so many find they do.

There are some people who are more likely to develop addiction than others and, broadly speaking, they are those who also have issues with the following:

- **Developing self-control** – this is particularly relevant for those in adolescence who may have more issues with impulse control or who have not had appropriate boundaries put in place by parents. A family background that has been very rigid and strict is more likely to result in someone who either rebels or finds it difficult to set boundaries for themselves.
- **Managing difficult feelings** – children learn how to express their emotions from watching their parents, which means that people who had poor role models are less likely to know how to appropriately and healthily express themselves. So families where emotions were either kept hidden, or were expressed dramatically or dangerously, are more likely to foster addiction.
- **Secrets and shame** – shame is the common denominator in almost all addictions, and when a child is brought up to feel shame about themselves, they are more likely to get caught in shame-based issues in adulthood. There is also a correlation between secretive families and

addiction, with 41.79 per cent describing this as their experience, in the survey undertaken for *Understanding and treating sex addiction* (Hall 2012). When a child has been brought up to keep secrets, then it is much easier as an adult to live a double life.

• **Poor sex education** – all of us need guidance and education in order to make choices for ourselves. When sex education has been poor or absent this can lead to increased feelings of shame around sex, increased experimentation and poor decision-making.

• **Adolescent loneliness** – using masturbation for comfort is a common and natural pastime for most adolescents, but if a young person feels isolated from others and unable to fit in with peers, they are less likely to develop other coping strategies and learn to turn to people for comfort.

Trauma-induced addiction

The links between trauma and addiction are well known and have been discussed in addiction circles for many years (Carruth 2006). Addiction may, on some occasions, be directly triggered by a traumatic event, for example, bereavement, physical assault, sudden illness or witnessing a violent or life-threatening act. Sometimes a traumatic event, or events, occur in childhood, and sex becomes a way of coping with the subsequent emotional and physical fallout. Significant trauma can also have a direct impact on the structure of the brain, and the repetitive nature of the compulsive behaviour can become a way of soothing a hyperactive amygdala and limbic system and reduce symptoms of hyper-arousal and hypo-arousal (Fisher 2007; Fowler 2006).

Someone with a trauma-induced addiction is most likely to use the behaviour to self-soothe difficult emotions, and the chosen behaviour may in some way replicate the initial trauma. There has been increasing evidence that some compulsive fetish behaviours and paraphilias are linked to previous trauma. The opponent-process theory of acquired motivation (Soloman 1980) describes how a negative emotion or experience can be reframed as a positive in order to rewrite the script. For example, someone who was bullied and humiliated as a child might pay a dominatrix to sexually arouse them by doing likewise, hence turning trauma into triumph (Birchard 2011).

Traumas come in many different shapes and sizes. Some are very obvious, such as violent assaults or childhood abuse, but others are more subtle or may have occurred very early in childhood before language developed, and hence be impossible to remember in words. If someone with addiction has experienced any of the following, then their addiction is almost certainly linked. Furthermore, they will almost certainly benefit from additional therapy to resolve these trauma issues in addition to recovery work.

- **Abuse** – abuse may be either emotional, physical or sexual, and may come from within or outside of the family of origin. When abuse has happened within the family then there will almost definitely be attachment issues as well. Research statistics vary in the amount of abuse present in the histories of people with sex addiction. In *Don't call it love*, Carnes cites 97 per cent, emotional abuse; 83 per cent, sexual abuse; and 71 per cent, physical. In my survey, 38 per cent reported emotional abuse; 17 per cent, sexual abuse; and 16 per cent, physical abuse. This may of course in part be dependent on the survey type and the clinical and subjective definition of abuse. Interestingly those who had been through therapy in my survey reported higher incidences of abuse, which perhaps indicates that some abuse is normalised or denied.
- **Assault** – an assault might best be described as a severe isolated incident of abuse, usually violent, that may be physical or sexual. As with abuse, that may happen within the home but more often it will be an attack by someone outside of the family. An assault may be physical, with or without a weapon, or be sexual, most commonly rape. In my survey, 16 per cent had been physically or sexually assaulted. For most people, an assault will be terrifying, but some, especially those with a history of abuse, may normalise the experience or explain it away by saying they were 'asking for it'. Someone who has survived an assault may use sex not only as a way of managing the emotional impact but also as a way of soothing the physical memories.
- **Other shocks to the system** – we all have to come to terms with losing a loved one at some time in our life, but when it happens prematurely, as happened for 21 per cent of survey respondents (Hall 2012), losing a parent, sibling or young partner, can be experienced as a trauma. Sudden illness or disability can also be experienced as a trauma, whether that is to oneself or a loved one. Another trauma that is often forgotten is the impact on children of witnessing domestic violence.

Attachment-induced addiction

'Addiction is an attachment disorder' is a common refrain among addiction specialists and this is undoubtedly true in a significant number of cases (Flores 2004). When a child forms a secure attachment to their primary caregiver they are more likely to grow into an adult with positive self-esteem who is able to tolerate and manage strong emotions and mild trauma (Potter-Efron 2006). But if positive parenting has been unreliable or absent, a child is more likely to fear negative feelings and turn to an addiction for comfort during times of trouble rather than to a person.

Someone with an attachment-induced addiction will often be unconsciously using their behaviour as a way of soothing relational pain such as fears of rejection or suffocation, loneliness or low self-esteem. For partners, this can be difficult to understand, especially if your relationship had always been close and loving. Ironically, sex addiction is often used to alleviate fears of losing the relationship, while increasing the likelihood that their fears will be realised.

Healthy attachment starts from the moment we are born. A newborn baby 'attaches' to their primary caregiver, usually mum, for survival. As the child grows they continue to need that attachment in order to develop healthily. When a child feels nurtured and cared for they have the courage to explore their world, knowing that safety is just a cry away. This attachment is important for emotional as well as physical development. When a child is still in the pre-verbal stage, they need a parent who is empathically attuned to their needs. And as they learn to talk, they need a parent who is encouraging and responsive to their efforts to communicate. Without this, a child may not develop the necessary skills to recognise and communicate their needs to others appropriately or to recognise and respond to the needs of others – including sexual needs. But the effects are not just emotional, they are also biologically imprinted and affect the developing brain. This means that those with early attachment difficulties may also be physically predisposed to addiction (Hall 2013).

Childhood attachment issues can arise from a number of different parenting scenarios, namely:

- **Absent** – if a child is physically separated from a parent for adoption or fostering or through bereavement, then there will inevitably be at least a short period of time when good parenting is absent.
- **Abusive** – as discussed under trauma, someone who experienced abusive parenting did not grow up in an environment that a child needs in order to thrive and learn how to manage their emotions in a healthy and appropriate way.
- **Negligent** – while not overtly abusive, negligent parenting leaves a child feeling fearful, as they are never fully sure how a parent will respond. A negligent parent is inconsistent; they may be caring and attentive one minute, and absent, rejecting or cruel the next. Usually this is the result of a parent's own personal problems and they may be aware of their inadequacies and be apologetic to the child.
- **Inadequate** – the term 'inadequate parenting' can be used to describe a childhood situation where parents were unavailable or unresponsive due to extenuating circumstances, for example, physical or emotional illness of themselves or another child, parental separation or divorce,

being a victim of domestic violence, extreme poverty, or simply because of naivety.

Someone who has an attachment-induced addiction is most likely to grow up into someone who has difficulties in their adult relationships. Certain styles of relating can develop, and often these play out in the couple's dynamics throughout their time together. There is much more on this in Chapter 9.

How addiction is maintained and reinforced

Now we've looked at how sex addiction begins, it is important to understand how it is maintained and reinforced. As you will no doubt be aware, or will have experienced yourself, most of us will be attracted to an addictive substance or process at some stage in our lives, but most of us are able to pull back. We recognise within us a point where our indulgence is becoming problematic and we either curtail our habit or stop altogether. We know that although we may be enjoying what we're doing, it's either already beginning to harm us, or it will do at some point in the future.

There are a number of reasons why this doesn't happen for people with an addiction. As we've already explored, this is partly due to brain development and chemistry. The more someone uses a chemical or a process to produce a dopamine high, the less able the brain is to produce enough through its own resources. The more effective the high, the stronger the memory and the brain's orientation towards seeking it again. For a trauma survivor, the brain becomes hypersensitive to arousal and therefore more vulnerable to seeking external opioids for self-soothing.

There are also significant emotional, psychological and societal influences that both maintain and reinforce the addictive behaviour. And each of these factors form what is known as the cycle of addiction – a cycle that, if not recognised, can keep someone unknowingly, and indefinitely, trapped.

The six-phase cycle of sex addiction

The six-phase cycle shown below, in Figure 2.2, is the cycle that I have developed over the years of my practice that helps clients recognise how their addiction continues to maintain itself through their behaviours, thoughts and emotions. The length of each phase, and the length of time between each phase, varies from individual to individual, as does the content, but everyone has a cycle. There is more on the cycle of addiction in *Understanding and treating sex addiction* (Hall 2012), but, in brief, the stages can be summarised as below:

1   **Dormant** – this is the phase where the addiction is temporarily in remission, but underlying issues, whether opportunity, trauma or attachment induced, remain unresolved. Life may appear 'normal', but it is only a matter of time before a trigger occurs.

2   **Trigger** – a trigger is an event, opportunity, bodily sensation, emotion, or thought process that activates the behaviour. Almost anything can be a trigger, but most commonly it will be a sexual opportunity or a negative emotion such as anxiety, anger, depression, sadness, boredom, loneliness or frustration.

3   **Preparation** – the preparation phase can vary considerably in length, from just a few minutes to turn on a computer, to many weeks of planning an affair. This phase includes practical preparation, such as the where, when and how, as well as psychological strategies to create the environment where acting out can be tolerated and/or enjoyed.

4   **Acting out** – for some, 'acting out' is a single event, such as visiting a sex worker, which may last just a few minutes, whereas for others it may be a week-long binge of pornography use. Some describe it as a highpoint that brings euphoria and relief, but for others the accompanying relief is purely about getting the deed over and done with so they can finally begin their descent back to the comfort of the dormant phase.

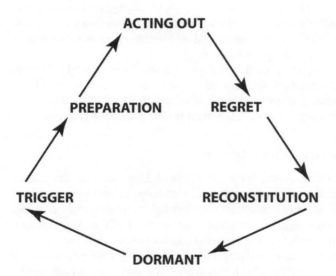

Figure 2.2 The six-phase cycle of addiction

5   **Regret** – depending on the consequences of acting out, the impact on
    personal values and someone's commitment to change, the regret phase
    may be experienced as little more than a momentary 'oops', or as weeks
    of despair, shame and self-loathing.

6   **Reconstitution** – during the reconstitution phase, life is either con-
    sciously or unconsciously put back together again. It may be a time for
    rebuilding self-esteem, covering tracks and/or renewing resolutions not
    to act out again.

How sex addiction is treated

Unfortunately there is still a lot of misunderstanding about sex addiction
within the professional communities, and very little training, which means
that some therapists and medical professionals treat sex addiction very
poorly indeed. If your partner has already been for treatment, or is currently
thinking of doing so, then do make sure they are seeing someone who is
professionally qualified and trained. The UK benchmark for sex addiction
training and professional standards is the ATSAC (Association for the
Treatment of Sexual Addiction and Compulsivity) so any therapist should
at least be a member, and ideally trained on an ATSAC-validated course.

In total, there are six treatment objectives for overcoming sex addiction
and they can be remembered by the rather cheesy acrostic 'UR-CURED'.
Please let me assure you that it is purely coincidental that the first letters of
each objective spell out UR-CURED. I have tried to come up with an
alternative, but have failed. UR-CURED is not intended to be a trite sales
claim or marketing gimmick, but something that will be easy to remember.
Hopefully the 'naffness' will make it especially memorable!

> **U**nderstand sex addiction
> **R**educe shame
> **C**ommit to recovery
> **U**nderstand and personalise the cycle of addiction
> **R**esolve underlying issues
> **E**stablish relapse prevention strategies
> **D**evelop a healthy life

Understand sex addiction

First and foremost it is essential that someone suffering with sex addiction
'understands' the problem they are facing. Education should be a prerequisite
for any treatment approach, especially in our current social climate where
there continues to be so much misunderstanding. Until someone knows that

sex addiction is a genuine health condition, not something invented to excuse poor impulse control, infidelity or an insatiable sex drive, they will be unable to move on to the next stage of treatment.

Reduce shame

Many partners understandably want their other halves to feel shame – but shame can significantly increase the chances of relapse, whereas guilt can be a positive motivator for change. Guilt is an emotion triggered by conscience about one's behaviour, whereas shame is a negative emotion about the self. Guilt says 'I did something bad' whereas shame says 'I am a bad person' (Gilliland *et al.* 2011).

Shame is common to people with sex addiction, not necessarily shame about the behaviours per se, but shame about the dependency and the pain they've caused others. But while shame continues, many feel they're unworthy, or incapable of change. Part of the therapeutic process is to change shame to guilt so the addict can feel empowered to change, and this is more successful within a group of other sufferers than in individual therapy. Some partners struggle initially with the idea of shame reduction, but once they're confident that a good therapist will ensure shame is replaced with guilt and commitment to change, then views can change.

Commit to recovery

Many people first seek help for sex addiction because their world, or at least their relationship, is falling apart and the key motivator is survival. That is fine as a starting place, but recovery takes time, and for some it's a commitment that lasts a lifetime. Overcoming any addiction isn't just about learning how to stop, it also means working on deeper issues and developing a life free of addiction.

It is impossible to say how long that process will take, as it depends on the severity of the addiction and the resources and motivation of the individual, but it will most likely include both individual and group therapy. Furthermore, evidence suggests that regular, ongoing attendance at a support group, such as a 12-step meeting, can significantly aid recovery (Krentzman 2007). All of this has an impact on partners and can influence the decision about whether to stay or leave. There is more on this in Chapter 9.

Understand and personalise the cycle of addiction

Everybody is unique and therefore every addiction is unique. There are of course many commonalities as we have previously explored, but in order to overcome addiction, it is crucial to fully understand the unique elements that make up an individual's sex addiction cycle. It means understanding the unmet needs and unresolved issues of the dormant phase; identifying triggers; recognising the cognitive distortions that happen during the preparation phase; understanding the function of the addiction in the acting out phase; and becoming aware of how the regret and reconstitution phases are experienced and managed.

Resolve underlying issues

Unless the underlying functions of addiction are identified and addressed, someone with an addiction will continue to act out. Relapse prevention strategies may help to stop and 'stay stopped' for a while, but without resolving the deeper unmet needs and issues, recovery will be reduced to pure willpower, and the sufferer has no choice but to 'white-knuckle' it. This stage of therapy may be the longest, the slowest and the most painful, as the root of addiction is exposed, examined and pulled out.

Establish relapse prevention strategies

Relapse prevention strategies are a part of treatment that needs to be woven throughout the work. Some people arrive for therapy having already stopped their behaviour, and their most urgent need and request is to establish strategies that will help them to remain stopped. Others may have experienced the shock of discovery as such a traumatic experience that they are convinced they will not relapse, at least not for many months or even years. Whatever the situation, it's important to understand that relapse prevention is a part of the treatment programme and that the process of establishing these strategies will be an ongoing part of not just therapy, but life.

Develop a healthy life

Someone once wisely said that 'recovery is not about learning to manage addiction, but learning to manage life'. For many people with an addiction, whether to drugs, alcohol, gambling or sex, their addiction has become an integral part of their lifestyle and therefore stopping means changing the way they live. Most people with an addiction benefit from making changes to how they relate to others, how they spend their time and looking at their goals for the future.

What 'recovery' looks like

Overcoming sex addiction is not a one-off event, but a lifetime commitment. Addiction is not an illness that can be cured, but an affliction that has to be lived with. A useful analogy is to think of someone who has been diagnosed with diabetes. If you're lucky and the condition is mild, then keeping the illness at bay may take little more than changes in diet and self-awareness. But for some, it means significant lifestyle changes and taking ongoing medication. Addiction is similar. Recovery for some means making some basic changes and then ensuring there is occasional monitoring to ensure the condition doesn't worsen and the changes are still effective. For others, recovery means significant changes to daily routines and regular attendance at support groups and engagement in recovery routines. For both, recovery is an active, ongoing process. What that means on a day-to-day basis depends on each individual, but the impact on partners can be significant.

3   Why sex addiction hurts partners so much

Sex addiction hurts partners in a way that no other addiction can. It is not uncommon to hear partners say 'I could cope with any other addiction', or those who are already supporting a partner with chemical addiction say 'I would rather you went back to drinking'. Discovering your partner has sex addiction is traumatic because it evokes all of the most destructive ingredients of personal pain – betrayal, sexual infidelity, deceit and shame. It also combines the well-known devastation of an affair with the torment and challenges of addiction.

There are three main reasons why sex addiction hurts so much. The first is the social stigma associated with the condition, the second is the painful and often drawn-out process of disclosure or discovery, and the third is the assumptions and misunderstandings made by some well-meaning friends and untrained therapists. We will explore these in detail, in reverse order.

Common assumptions and misunderstandings

Some relationship therapists have tried to work with a partner's pain by treating it as an infidelity, but it is so much more than that. Similarly, addiction professionals have brought all their years of experience of working with partners of chemical addictions to the table when helping sex addiction partners, but the same principles often do not apply. Regrettably many partners have had insult added to injury by experts who have failed to recognise the uniqueness of a sex addict's partner's pain.

Friends and family can also fall into the trap of thinking they understand what a partner is going through, but often the quick conclusions drawn in an attempt to offer love and support make partners feel worse.

It's like an affair

Partners of sex addicts can feel a profound sense of betrayal that is similar to the feelings experienced by people who have been betrayed by an affair, but there are essential differences that make this comparison unhelpful.

First, affairs are nearly always a symptom of a problem within the relationship or are a consequence of a significant relationship breakdown. There are of course exceptions to this, but when one partner has an affair it normally results in a process of scrutinising the relationship and exploring the role that both partners may have played in creating the environment within which the affair could happen. If the couple is unable to agree on the source of the problem they will usually separate or they work together to rebuild trust and resolve the underlying issues.

Sex addiction, as with any addiction, is not a couple problem. Relationship difficulties may contribute to the problem, but they most certainly are not a cause. If an alcoholic announced, 'if it wasn't for our relationship I wouldn't get drunk', they would be rightly accused of not taking responsibility for their behaviour and not acknowledging the severity of their problem. And they could almost certainly be challenged that there were many times they were drunk when the relationship was OK. This leads us to the second essential difference.

There is no 'before'. In almost every case, sex addiction pre-dates the relationship, so when a well-meaning couple counsellor asks 'how was your relationship when you first got together?', it is irrelevant. As we saw in the last chapter, most partners have to face the harsh reality that they have always been with an addict. Even the very best honeymoon days of the relationship were unknowingly shadowed by the addiction. In every other relationship crisis, there is a 'before' to hold on to or head back to, but not in the case of addiction.

As well as there being no 'before', there may also be no 'after'. When a couple has experienced an affair they can (hopefully) look forward to the day when they can put the pain behind them and move on, perhaps even forgetting what happened. But living with someone in recovery from addiction means that there will always be reminders. That might mean ongoing therapy, going to meetings, engaging in relapse prevention strategies, avoiding certain triggers, etc. It's unlikely, at least for a few years, that a week will go by when you're not in some way or another reminded that your partner is in recovery from addiction. But as I hope you'll see as you continue to read this book, that's not necessarily a bad thing.

You'll get over it

At best, this is a shallow platitude, at worst it denies the pain of having to decide whether to stay with a partner in recovery or end the relationship. As we said in the previous paragraph and will continue to explore, staying with a partner in recovery is challenging for many partners and aiming to 'get over it' can actually be quite damaging as it can lull couples into a false sense of security and make the risk of relapse harder to identify and avoid.

If they do decide to separate, many partners are still haunted by many of the same self-doubts as the partners who choose to stay – doubts that can go on to impact future relationships.

Once an addict, always an addict

For most people, recovering from addiction is a lifetime commitment, but that doesn't mean it's a constant challenge or a painful process, and it most certainly does not mean that the person with the addiction hasn't changed. On the contrary, many people who are in recovery would say that they have made profound personal changes that have significantly improved every area of their life.

How an addict feels about being in recovery will have an impact on the partner. Similarly, how a partner feels about living with someone in recovery will impact the addict. You can either see recovery as a burden or as a gift. You can focus on the restrictions it puts on your life, or you can see all the new doors that are opening up. I know it's a cliché, but discovering and acknowledging addiction is a learning opportunity. If you do decide to give your addicted partner a second, or even third or fourth, chance then the consequence may be that you are both able to appreciate more and work harder than those who have never faced such challenges.

Partners are 'all' co-dependent

Co-dependency is a term that is widely used and even more widely misunderstood. The term became popular in the late 1970s and was used to describe the partners of alcoholics whose caring and protecting behaviours were unwittingly perpetuating and enabling their spouse's addiction. The term quickly spread to the partners of any addict who offered ongoing care and support rather than forcing their partners to face the consequences of their behaviour, which might mean the breakdown of the relationship. It was felt that anyone who stayed with an alcoholic, drug addict or compulsive gambler, in spite of the damaging consequences to their own lives, was a co-dependent. So when the sex addiction label became popularised in the US in the 1980s by addiction professionals the co-dependency label was automatically adopted. In 2009 the groundbreaking book *Your sexually addicted spouse* (Steffens and Means) rightly challenged the co-dependency label, and since then there has been growing recognition that it frequently does not fit, or at least, not in the traditional understanding of the term in the case of chemical addiction.

Unlike other addictions, it is perfectly possible to stay in a relationship with a sex addict for many, many years and have absolutely no awareness of the problem. Even if there are hints of problematic behaviours, such as spending long periods of time on the computer or working late at the office, there are many other rational explanations other than sex or porn addiction. However, once a partner does know that their partner is an addict, there is a risk that co-dependency may develop. Especially if there has been a history of compulsive caregiving in the past such as looking after an addicted or dependent parent or child.

For many partners of sex addicts, there is no co-dependency. And for those who do identify themselves as co-dependent, it should in no way detract from the work of overcoming the feelings of trauma and betrayal. There is more on identifying, avoiding and overcoming co-dependency in Chapter 8.

Sex addicts can't do intimacy

This is another of those blanket statements that can be especially damaging for partners. Most partners find themselves wracked with doubt about the true quality of their relationship before disclosure or discovery. To be told by a professional that sex addicts can't do intimacy can leave many partners feeling that the whole of their relationship was meaningless and a charade. Those who may have previously experienced themselves as loved and cherished by their partner can find themselves questioning their ability to know what real love feels like.

Before the days of internet porn, a high percentage of sex addicts were people who had come from backgrounds with inadequate or abusive parenting. The result of their childhood experiences often left them finding it very difficult to have meaningful and intimate relationships in adult life. These were the sex addicts written about in the seminal works of writers such as Patrick Carnes and Eli Coleman, who were often using their acting out behaviours as a way of avoiding, or minimising, the pain of intimacy within their primary relationships. But as we've already discussed in earlier chapters, the profile of someone with sex or porn addiction has changed considerably over the years and there are now many, many people who are able to have full intimate and loving relationships, and act out. For some of these addicts, the acting out behaviour may slowly erode the intimacy and connection in their relationships as they increasingly withdraw into the secrecy and shame of their addiction. But it does not mean that they are incapable of it.

Another common refrain is that addicts are looking for intensity rather than intimacy, and for most this is true. But it doesn't necessarily mean that they're looking for intensity in preference to intimacy.

Sex is a complex experience with many variables. Each sexual experience will be unique, and the goal of the experience, which may be unconscious, will be to meet a variety of needs. Some will seek an intense erotic experience, some intimacy and connection, some fun and play, others excitement and adventure. Many people with sex addiction will always enjoy the intimacy of sex in their primary relationship, but may be splitting off their needs for other types of sexual experience in acting out.

Sex addicts are a risk to children

When you find out that someone's sexual behaviour is 'out of their control' it is understandable that a parent may have concerns about the impact it could have on children. But there is no evidence to suggest that sex or porn addiction reduces someone's capacity to responsibly look after their children.

With other addictions there are fears of physical and mental impairment while under the influence of drugs or alcohol, and there is a subsequent comedown or hangover that may accompany a period of acting out or relapse. But there is no similar impact on functioning with sex or porn addiction. Whatever your values may be about the morality of someone's sexual behaviours, there is no reason to believe that it makes them a bad parent or a risk to children.

Regrettably there is an assumption by some of the public and some uneducated professionals that sex addiction is in some way akin to sexual offending. But that would be like saying that every alcoholic is a criminal. There are of course some people with addictions who break the law when under the influence, or to feed their addiction, but they are a minority. Similarly there are some people with sex addiction who have engaged in offending behaviours, and if those offences have included people under the age of 18 then it would be prudent to undertake a professional risk assessment. But except in these rare circumstances, there is no reason to assume that anybody, let alone a child, is at risk.

This myth is a particular burden on partners who are parents who want to stay in the relationship with someone in recovery. On top of the fears and shame that addiction brings, the additional fear of judgement by ignorant outsiders can be especially damaging. Of course, it also impacts the children as well who deserve to love, and be loved by, both parents, whether or not they continue to stay in a relationship together or become a separated family.

You must have known (at least on some level)

Even if this isn't actually said, it is often implied in the comments and questions raised by friends and professionals alike when partners talk about the discovery or disclosure of sex addiction. This statement usually says much more about the speaker than it does about the partner, and demonstrates their shock and disbelief. A more helpful, and more accurate, statement would be 'it's hard to comprehend that someone can act out in the ways they have and keep it so completely hidden'. But in reality, that is precisely what happens in sex addiction.

The assumption that a partner 'must' have had some inkling is supported further when hindsight is confused with unconscious knowing, or what some addiction professionals might even call denial. For example, when a partner reflects on their past and says 'he did seem to spend a huge amount of time on his computer' or 'he said he couldn't be contacted abroad because his phone didn't work there' and they now realise they must have been acting out, that is most likely hindsight. Hindsight develops when we look back at an event of the past with new knowledge from today and create a different, often more accurate, picture. We all have times when we have experienced hindsight, be that an adolescent's secret party, a friend's relationship breakdown or a workplace making redundancies. The fact that you can see clearly now does not mean that you were in denial, or should have known, earlier.

When professionals, therapists or friends interpret hindsight as unconscious knowing it can add further shame and self-doubt to partners. It is natural for partners to wonder if they should or could have seen the signs, but often there are none. What's more, partners are usually busy getting on with their own lives and have no reason to assume their partner is doing anything untoward. Unlike other addictions, sex addiction is invisible and can exist and flourish while remaining completely and total concealed.

He/she is not who you thought they were

In many ways, this is the opposite of the above and is frequently offered as words of encouragement and support. The intention of the statement is often to reduce a partner's shame by saying 'you wouldn't be with them if you'd known who they were'. While it may be true in part, statements such as this can increase feelings of shame and self-doubt because it says that you made a mistake about the whole person, rather than not knowing about the addiction. So everything about the addict is brought into question – their personality and character, their relationships with others, their history, and their likes and dislikes.

Thinking that you did not know your partner can leave partners feeling bereft of everything they've known and enjoyed in the past. Flooded with endless questions, partners may wonder if they were really loved at all. Was everything a sham and a lie?

It seems to be much easier to recognise chemical addictions as an illness or a condition that someone has, rather than a problem that someone is. If someone develops alcoholism, their life before the addiction is not brought into question. But when someone has sex addiction, their whole being is now open to debate. In reality, sex and porn addiction are like the other addictions in so much as it's a problem that someone has, not who someone is. What partners didn't know was that they were living with someone who has sex addiction. But that doesn't mean that everything else they knew about them was untrue. It is perfectly possible (and very common) for someone with sex or porn addiction to be a loving partner, a devoted mother or father, a pillar of the community, a trustworthy, kind, sensitive and moral person. Everything you thought they were was true. But there is now an additional piece that you didn't know about – a piece you may not want to live with.

You're overreacting

Thankfully there are very few friends or professionals who would say this outright, but sometimes misguided attempts to make the problem feel more manageable have the same effect.

Most commonly, a well-meaning friend will minimise what has happened by making broad generalisations based on their experiences and their perception of societal norms. Interestingly, what is perceived as 'normal' varies widely depending on the gender and orientation of the partner and the person with the addiction. So, typically, a male addict's behaviour may be minimised as 'just what men do'. Or if you're in a gay relationship your assumption or definition of fidelity may be challenged as 'not realistic'. Partners of female sex addicts find their problem minimised in a different way, as friends may suggest that they're 'lucky to be with such a sexual women'. Indeed, male partners often have the hardest time getting understanding from their male friends.

Another way in which partners' pain is minimised is when the media and so-called professionals dismiss the notion that sex and porn addiction exist, or they misdiagnose or mislabel yet another wayward celebrity to excuse their indiscretion. It is profoundly hurtful for partners to read that sex or porn addiction is not real when they are the innocent victims of the painful truth and reality.

Sex addiction is unlike any other addiction because it violates the very core of a couple's intimate relationship. At the time of writing this book, it is still something that is commonly misunderstood within our culture. So not only do partners have to experience the personal pain and betrayal of sex addiction, they often also feel betrayed by professionals and society.

How the discovery or disclosure process affects reaction

There are many different ways that partners find out about sex addiction, and the way it is discovered, or disclosed, directly affects how much it hurts. Some partners find out all at once in one dramatic event, either in a confession or by finding physical evidence. Others have their suspicions for many months or even years and it is through hard detective work that the reality is finally revealed. Others endure numerous painful confessions or discoveries, each time being told that there is nothing else to be shared, each time discovering they've been lied to again as more and more of the truth leaks out.

The survey showed that partners' most common ways of finding out about sex addiction are shown in Table 3.1 below.

Below are described the most common ways that partners find out, and how each scenario impacts the emotional response. You may think that some are better than others, but they all carry their own unique agonies.

The sledgehammer blow

This describes how it feels when a partner suddenly discloses sex addiction or the truth is in some other way instantly revealed, which was the harsh reality for 17 per cent of survey respondents. For some it is discovering physical evidence, either emails or an online profile, or video clips or websites. For a few, it is being told either by their partner or one of their lovers or someone else who knew before them. For a small, but devastated, minority, it is by contracting a sexually transmitted infection (STI).

Shock is undoubtedly the biggest and most powerful reaction to this kind of disclosure and it is often experienced as a trauma. There is no time for psychological or emotional preparation and hence partners can find themselves feeling especially confused and frightened by the discovery.

Table 3.1 Partners survey – how did you find out?

Answered: 115 Skipped: 11		
Answer choices	*Responses*	
Partner confessed	17%	19
Someone else told me	3%	3
I discovered 'evidence'	77%	88
I dragged it out of my partner	16%	18
Total respondents: 115		

Furthermore, the disclosure or discovery will almost always have been forced by some external event onto the person with the addiction, which means they may be in the weakest position to offer support. While the shock may be greater than any of the other types of disclosure, the one saving grace is that everything is out and over all at once.

The drip, drip, drip disclosure

This is probably the most common disclosure process, as the person with the addiction tells the truth of their acting out over an extended period of time. Few addicts can bear the pain they cause to their partners and hence they may let the story out in dribs and drabs, waiting for a new reality to be absorbed before revealing another. While on some levels this may feel to the addict as if it's the kindest thing to do, for partners it often feels like they have only just begun to piece together their broken emotional life when another blow is struck.

Partners who experience this type of disclosure (60.87 per cent in the survey) are the ones most likely to feel fear and anxiety, as they have no idea when, or if, another revelation will come. A spouse may swear that they have told all, but then more comes out. Partners may find themselves fearing coming to terms with the pain, lest that simply makes space for more.

The drip, drip, drip exposure

Similar to the drip, drip, drip disclosure, this is a process that can be dragged out for many weeks or months. But the discoveries are due to the partner's persistent and ongoing efforts to discover the truth, rather than a result of the addict's disclosure. Partners who have found out in this way have often been digging for details either overtly, or covertly, for a long period of time before they feel that they have anything vaguely resembling the full story. In the survey, 77 per cent said they 'discovered evidence' and 16 per cent said they 'dragged it out of their partner'.

Partners who find out in this way are often the angriest. Their spouses have often lied to them on countless occasions, swearing that there is nothing else to be known. These partners will have spent long periods of time feeling restless and suspicious, neglecting other meaningful parts of their lives because of their desire to get to the bottom of what's going on. Suspicion is likely to continue long after the full story has been revealed, and these partners are likely to find it hardest to rebuild trust as they continue to assume that their spouse is more intent on protecting themselves than telling the truth.

The detective breakthrough

These partners have also had to find out the truth through their own detective efforts. Many will have had suspicions for a long time that things weren't quite right. That might be because of a partner's secretive behaviour or because they have changed over a period of time and no longer act the same in the relationship. But unlike the drip, drip exposure, the discovery comes all in large chunks and may culminate in one dramatic breakthrough. In the survey, 22 per cent found out the truth over a matter of weeks.

Shock and relief are the two most common feelings for these partners, but also feelings of anger that it has taken so long for them to find out what's going on. The yo-yoing of emotions between anger, shock and relief can leave these partners confused about their own feelings and struggling to decide how to move on.

The pain of gradual disclosure is not purely psychological, but also physiological. As we will explore further in the next chapter, discovering your partner has sex addiction is a trauma, and trauma affects the way our brains work. Evidence has shown that our brains need an absolute minimum of 30 days of calm to begin to heal itself, and hence repeated disclosures or discoveries that happen close together further compound the trauma and delay the recovery process (Turnbull 2011).

The pain of social stigma

All addictions struggle with a social stigma, be it alcohol, drugs or gambling, but none are as bad as sex addiction. When I'm delivering training to professionals I always start with a word association game to help them consider how sex addiction is viewed. Common words include sad, selfish, a player, greedy, pervert, desperate, lonely, weird, out-of-control, loser, and grandiose.

These are all labels that affect not only the person with the addiction but also the partner. It's a heavy load to bear.

In the survey, I asked how partners felt about the sex addiction label before discovery, in the early weeks after the discovery, and now. Table 3.2 shows the results.

For some partners there is an additional layer of social stigma and shame. According to the survey undertaken for *Understanding and treating sex addiction*, nearly 30 per cent of heavy porn users will have looked at an illegal image, such as bestiality or someone under the age of 18. Other offline addicts may have engaged in voyeurism or exhibitionism. In other words, in one way or another many people with sex addiction find their behaviours have escalated into offending, and those who have been caught may be facing

Table 3.2 Partners survey – sex addiction is a 'real' problem

	Answered: 96 Skipped: 30					
	I'd never thought about it	*Didn't believe at all*	*Believed a little, but was cynical*	*Definitely believed, but thought 'real' cases were probably rare*	*Totally believed it was a real problem*	*Total*
Before discovering your partner's behaviour	46% 44	5% 5	23% 22	17% 16	9% 9	96
In the early days/weeks before discovering your partner's behaviour	3% 3	12% 11	27% 26	31% 29	27% 26	95
Now	1% 1	2% 2	6% 6	12% 11	79% 75	95

prosecution. This can be especially difficult for partners to cope with and understand, and some find themselves feeling isolated from other partners whose mates are not burdened with the additional label of 'sex offender'.

There is not enough space in this book to cover the additional needs of partners of sex offending addicts, especially those who may be parents with child protection procedures in place. But it is important to know that, more often than not, offending behaviours are a symptom and escalation of addiction, not an indicator of any kind of sexual preference. The addiction needs to be dealt with in the same way as any other kind of sex or porn addiction, and additional help and advice should also be sought.

Finally, one other significant difference between sex and porn addiction and other addictions is the woeful lack of professional help and resources. This situation is slowly beginning to change, but regrettably there are still many partners who find themselves feeling very, very alone.

Part II

Caring for partners' needs

'You can't stop the waves, but you can learn to surf'

Jon Kabat Zinn

The following five chapters are all about learning to SURF. Our first chapter offers insight and advice on how to 'Survive the trauma of discovering your partner has sex addiction'. Chapter 5 focuses on 'Understanding the cycle of reaction' that so many partners find themselves in as they try to recover from the trauma, and provides practical strategies for gaining greater control over unwanted emotional reactions. 'Repairing self-identity and self-esteem' is the subject for Chapter 6, and in Chapter 7 we'll explore how to 'Face the future', whether that's within the relationship or alone. Our final chapter in this section looks at the controversial subject of co-dependency and offers ways of identifying co-dependent thinking and behaviours and ways of overcoming it.

4 Surviving the trauma of discovery

Nothing prepares you for the discovery of sex addiction – absolutely nothing. In this chapter we will explore the first emotions that many partners experience and how to manage them, as well as how to deal with the urgent questions that so many partners struggle with.

The overwhelming first emotion experienced by almost every partner is shock. Even those who have been suspicious for a while are ill-prepared for the devastation of full disclosure, or discovery. Once the numbness of shock has worn off, many partners experience a flood of emotions that can feel totally overwhelming and, for many, the first six months are a roller-coaster ride of intense emotional pain, and little can be done except hang on.

There has been increasing awareness over recent years that the emotional responses of partners are similar to those who have experienced a trauma (Steffens and Rennie 2007) such as a sudden bereavement or assault. If those symptoms continue for more than six months, then it could be considered PTSD (post-traumatic stress disorder). If this describes you, then you may benefit from making an appointment to see a health professional, in addition to therapy, to discuss possible medication.

Common feelings

Below is a list of some common emotions experienced by partners. You may feel overwhelmed just reading them, and regrettably there are undoubtedly more.

anger
sadness
grief
loss
insecurity
shame
disgust

fear
shock
betrayal
humiliation
despair
helplessness
relief
annihilation
rage
disappointment
horror
numbness
frustrated
wounded
emptiness
remorse
isolation
threatened
overwhelmed
manipulation
abused
rejection
suspicion
doomed
sense of failure
disbelief
used
degradation
unloved
guilt

Some partners will have experienced all of these emotions, some just a few. You may have found that reading this list has triggered new feelings in you that you hadn't thought of or experienced before. If this is the case, then you may be feeling angry right now and perhaps thinking 'well I didn't feel humiliation until I read it in the list, but now I come to think about it I do feel humiliated'. This is a common experience of partners. One minute you may be feeling OK, and then a few seconds later something happens from out of the blue, maybe seeing or reading something, or a thought that seems to ping in from nowhere, and suddenly there's a flood of new emotion. This is what we refer to as 'being triggered' and we'll talk a lot more about that in the next chapter.

It's an unfortunate reality that if an emotion is inside you, it will at some time come out. It's just a question of what, or who, will make that emotion rise to the surface. So if, as you continue reading this book, you find yourself beginning to feel worse, rather than better, please do be assured that reading is not causing your pain, but rather uncovering it. Once uncovered, you can begin to manage the emotions, rather than fearing being ambushed by them.

One way of instantly feeling less overwhelmed by the many emotions you may experience is to recognise that most of them can be grouped under seven broad emotional categories. We will look at each of these categories one by one and consider some immediate coping strategies.

Shock

Shock is a normal response to a traumatic event, and discovering your partner is a sex addict is undoubtedly a traumatic event. Shock was experienced by 95 per cent of respondents in the survey, and 75 per cent described it as 'extreme'. Shock is also one of the hardest emotions to put into words. In some ways, all emotions can be hard to express, but shock is one that has a unique impact on our brains. When we experience shock, the thinking part of the brain switches off, which makes it especially hard to put feelings into words. Shock can be experienced as feeling numb, cold, empty or hollow. It is common for people to feel cut off from the real world, and some say they feel as if they've become an observer on their life. They can continue to function perfectly well, going to work; taking the children to school; running the home; but they feel detached from what they're doing and disconnected from people around them. Nothing feels real. In psychology terms, this is often referred to as dissociation.

Other common symptoms of shock are confusion (95 per cent), difficulty concentrating and disbelief (91 per cent). Even if a partner has confessed, or the evidence is undeniable, it is very common for partners to feel 'this cannot be happening to me'. These feelings of confusion and disbelief can also be very frightening. Because while one part of you is telling you that something awful has happened, there's another part that just wants to try and carry on as normal.

There are also physical symptoms of shock such as difficulty sleeping, changes in appetite, feeling shaky and jumpy, heart racing, breathlessness, muscle tension and tiredness, and an upset stomach. When a cluster of these physical symptoms occur together, we often refer to it as a panic attack.

While many of these emotions and physical experiences can be frightening, it is important to remember that these are very normal reactions to an abnormal event. Symptoms of shock normally only last for a few weeks, but the symptoms can continue if there are continuing traumas. As we will see in the next chapter, a lot of partners discover their partner's secret life over an extended period of time. Each disclosure or discovery can be experienced as another trauma, and with it comes another wave of shock.

Shock survival strategies

The most important thing to do if you're suffering from shock is to reach out to others. Isolation will only make your symptoms worse, so you need to find someone that you can talk to and share your feelings. If your partner is unable to support you right now, then try to think of a friend who you can trust to focus on your needs. If there is no one, then seek help from a professional or from one of the online self-help forums.

If you're suffering from shock, you also need to take extra care of yourself physically. Eating a healthy diet, watching your caffeine and alcohol intake, maintaining a fitness routine and trying, if you can, to get regular sleep will help you to manage the physical and psychological symptoms. There are also specific exercises called grounding exercises that can help you to manage feelings of dissociation and disconnection. What you need to do is make a conscious effort to reconnect with your body and your physical surroundings. For example, if you're sitting in a chair, then notice how the chair feels against your back and your bottom. Feel the warmth in your skin, the firmness against your body. Focus on your breathing – breathing in through your nose, and out through your mouth. You may find it helpful to count as you breathe and take twice as long to breathe out,

---

Knowing when to get medical help

If you've been experiencing any of the following symptoms for more than 6 weeks, you should make an appointment to see your doctor for further advice and support:

- significant changes in sleep or eating patterns;
- trouble concentrating on work or other regular tasks;
- regular overwhelming feelings of fear or panic;
- ongoing feelings of disconnection from other important people in your life or avoidance of people;
- flashbacks to painful feelings or images;
- regularly using drugs or alcohol to soothe symptoms;
- a desire to hurt yourself or thoughts about ending your life.

as in. For example, breathe in for a count of three, then out for a count of six. Notice the colours around you, the sounds in the room. Bring yourself back into your body and the present moment by using your senses to notice your surroundings.

If your symptoms feel out of control and are worrying you, or worrying those who love you, you would be wise to make an appointment to see your doctor. It may be that a course of medication will help you to manage your symptoms in the short term while you develop longer term coping strategies.

Anger

The amount of anger experienced is often proportional to the amount of deceit. In the survey, 97 per cent of respondents experienced anger, 66 per cent described it as 'extreme', 20 per cent as 'moderate' and 14 per cent as 'mild'. If your partner has been denying or lying about their behaviour for many years, then you may experience absolute rage when the truth is revealed. Rage is a horrible emotion that can be frightening and destructive to everyone around you. You may experience a desperate desire to punish your partner in an attempt to reduce your pain, but regrettably that rarely works. A desire for revenge is a common companion to rage, but all too often it backfires and can create even more pain and hurt, often taking in even more innocent victims in its wake.

A gentler expression of anger is frustration and irritation, nagging doubts and thoughts that keep going round and round, endless 'if only' statements that seem locked in your head with nowhere useful to go.

Anger can be directed in many different places. Most obviously and most commonly it is directed at the person with the addiction. But there can also be anger at others who were involved in the acting out, whether that is online partners or communities or sex workers. Anger may also be at wider society for not having prevented the sex addiction, or at the partner's parents or abuser who may be seen to have caused the problem in your spouse.

But perhaps the most destructive of all anger is when it's directed at the self. Many partners beat themselves up for not knowing they were living with a sex addict, or for not following their intuition or suspicions sooner and finding out earlier. Others find themselves trapped in self-blame and berate themselves for not doing something that would have prevented the addiction. From the survey, 85 per cent felt some degree of self-blame, most of whom described it as 'moderate' or 'mild'. When anger is directed at the self it can potentially lead to self-harm and suicidal feelings. A very concerning 27 per cent had either considered self-harming or had self-harmed and, even more worryingly, 29 per cent had contemplated taking their own life. These feelings can of course also be caused by overwhelming feelings of grief and despair. If this describes you, then you should make an appointment to see your doctor for additional help and support.

Managing anger

First and foremost, anger needs to be understood and accepted. There is nothing wrong with feeling anger and rage, but you do need to think about how you express it. When anger is expressed in an unhealthy way, it can be destructive and damaging and cause even more pain and upset to yourself and others. No matter how angry you may be feeling, you need to think about how you can express those feelings in a way that fits with your values and protects yourself and those that you love. Even though every sinew in your body may be screaming out for justice and vengeance, you do not want to do something in the heat of anger that you may regret for the rest of your life. Once something is said or done, it cannot be unsaid or undone.

Furthermore, when we get angry our bodies are flooded with chemicals that get us ready to fight or run away from a threat. We can cope with these chemicals for a time, but if your body stays angry these can end up in health issues such as headaches, high blood pressure, stomach problems and a lowered immune system. So finding better ways to manage anger will benefit your physical health, as well as your psychological and emotional wellbeing. Below are the three essential strategies for managing anger healthily.

1 DEVELOP AN EARLY WARNING SYSTEM

Anger often comes in tidal waves, flooding body and mind in seconds – or at least, that's how it may feel. But, in reality, there are often warning signs and once you become aware of those, you can stop anger before it overwhelms you.

Detecting those early signs means becoming more aware of what's going on in your head and what's going on in your body. Most likely your thoughts will be negative, angry thoughts. You may find yourself having an argument with someone in your head or telling someone what you think of them or how angry or upset you're feeling, quite possibly things that you wouldn't say out loud.

Some people aren't consciously aware of the thoughts that may be going round their head but notice instead that they're irritable and short of patience with things or people that wouldn't normally bother them. A classic sign is snapping at the children when they don't deserve it or getting angry with other drivers on the road.

In your body you may have sensations of tightness in your chest, shoulders or jaw, or you may clench your fists or grind your teeth. This may be accompanied by fidgeting and restlessness or finding yourself short of breath. You may also find yourself unable to sit still, maybe pacing up and down.

Once you've identified these signs you can begin to take immediate action to let it out.

2 LET IT OUT

Once you notice that your anger is building, it's time to take action. Some people like to let out their anger verbally, some physically, and some both. Letting out your anger verbally means making the space to vent your anger and frustrations with a trusted friend or professional. If there's no one around, you may find it helpful to write down your feelings or say them out loud where no one can hear you.

Many people also find it helpful to work off the excess adrenalin through exercise – going for a run or perhaps beating a cushion with your fists. But in order for this to be effective in reducing tension, rather than fuelling it, you need to make sure you continue your exertion to physical exhaustion.

The golden rule in anger management is to let it out, little and often. Think of a pan of water heating up on the stove. Don't wait until it hits boiling point before you remove it from the heat. As you feel yourself hotting up, find regular ways to let off steam and cool down to ensure that you don't boil over!

3 CHILL OUT

Once the thoughts and physical feelings are spent, you need to do something that will help your pulse rate to slow down, and your body and mind to relax. In the first instance you can simply focus on slowing your breathing, taking deep breaths and ensuring you exhale fully. You can also consciously release the tension in your muscles by shaking out your hands and limbs, sitting back into a comfortable chair and consciously relaxing your muscles.

To help you to maintain a calmer physical state, you could listen to calming music, go for a walk in nature, read a book or watch a favourite programme, or simply focus on something more pleasant. Once the anger has subsided, then, and only then, you will have the physical, psychological and emotional capacity to consider what you want to do.

Grief and despair

When you discover that your partner is a sex addict, the feelings of grief and loss can be immobilising. In the survey, 95 per cent of respondents felt relief, and nearly all described it as 'extreme'. Partners often feel that they have lost the solid ground on which their life was built. Their relationship is not what they thought it was, their spouse feels like a complete stranger, the world is no longer a place they recognise, and even the person they see in the mirror every morning does not look the same. Before the discovery you may have seen yourself as a strong and confident person, someone who was a good judge of character who knew what was going on in their world. But now that may be gone.

Grief is an aching emotion. It carries within it many other emotions that are a natural response to loss such as feelings of disbelief, anger, regret, longing and despair. Grief can also leave us feeling empty and depressed, or anxious and afraid. Grief is heartbreaking. As we read earlier, this may contribute to the 28 per cent of partners who have considered taking their own life. One of the hardest things about the grief caused by sex addiction is that the loss is abstract. Unlike bereavement or divorce, you have not lost a physical person. Some partners feel as though they've lost something that they never really had. They've lost a dream or a fantasy of what they had thought was reality. This kind of loss can be difficult to put into words and therefore harder to share with others. But the pain is just as real and it's important that you acknowledge that pain and don't tell yourself you're not entitled to it.

1 MAINTAIN PERSPECTIVE

It is also important not to let yourself lose the things in your life that are still real. You may have lost certain qualities within your relationship that you had assumed were there, such as fidelity and trust. But there are other qualities that nonetheless remain. Many partners find it hard to believe that anything in their relationship was good, but discovering addiction does not extinguish everything else. Imagine picking an apple from your fruit bowl and discovering that, on the hidden underside, there is a rotten bruise. That bruise does not mean that the rest of the apple is bad; there is only a part of it that you have lost.

Focusing on what you still have can be a positive response to grief. Take the time you need to cry and share your feelings with loved ones, but try and balance it with valuing and enjoying what you have and holding hope for the future.

2 ACKNOWLEDGE OPTIONS

Grief and despair rob us of any sense of control and agency that we feel we have over our lives. If you think about it logically, none of us really has any control. We never know when tragedy may strike, but while life is going along OK, we may 'feel' as though we're in control. Discovering sex addiction floors most people and can leave them feeling that they have no choice but be devastated, that they have nothing to look forward to in the future and no ability to choose how they move on. But, in reality, there are always options. They may be options that are more limited than you thought but, nonetheless, there are options.

Many relationships do survive sex addiction. Unfortunately there are no longitudinal statistics on this, but, in the survey, 90 per cent were still in a relationship. In Part III we talk more about the couple relationship and how you can work at rebuilding it and reclaiming sex and sexuality. There is also a chapter on deciding the future of the relationship. But as you'll see in Chapter 7 there is more to life than our relationships. Our primary relationship is very important to most of us, but there are other areas of life where we can find love, meaning and fulfilment. The option to care for others, to have friendships and positive family relationships is not taken away by addiction, and, for most, finding fulfilment and meaning in work and hobbies is also not affected – at least, not for ever.

A helpful exercise can be to take a sheet of paper and think about other key areas of your life such as friends; family; hobbies and pastimes; employment or voluntary work; and personal development. Make a note of what you enjoy and what you don't enjoy about these areas of your life and think about what options you have for improving them. In the short term at least, as you work through the grief of losing a partner, or losing the partner you thought you had, focusing on growth in these other areas can be source of comfort.

3 SOCIALISE

Grief and despair thrive on loneliness, so one of the most effective ways of managing these emotions is not to spend too much time alone. There are many different ways to socialise. Sometimes that may mean going out with friends who make you laugh and forget the problems at home, or it may be going out with a single close friend and sharing your feelings. It may mean being part of a support group of other partners and talking about your experiences, or indeed it may be going out and helping others with different difficulties to your own. It really doesn't matter what you do, as long as you don't spend all your time at home alone where feelings of despair can soon overwhelm.

Fear

Fear is one of the emotions that can be manifested in grief but it is also an emotion that can exist alone. Some partners can feel overwhelmed by fear or even 'terror', as one partner described it in the survey. Another described feeling 'a constant state of anxiety and fear'. Partners fear how, or if, they will cope, and what the future holds now they know what their partner has done. This is more likely to be the case if you have experienced previous traumas or loss in your life or if you are in a particularly vulnerable place right now. That vulnerability may be due to other life events such as illness or bereavement or it may be because you have recently given up work to look after children. Some partners feel torn between rage and fear, at times wanting to kick out their partner and never see them again, and then fearing how they would cope if they were left alone. There may also be practical fears about issues such as work, money, or contracting a sexually transmitted infection. For some, there are legal fears, especially if behaviours had crossed the line into offending, such as exhibitionism, voyeurism or viewing illegal pornography.

One way that fear can manifest itself is through intrusive thoughts and feelings of anxiety when being out in public. Some partners talk of feeling as though everyone is looking at them differently, or that they find themselves looking at everyone with suspicion, and wondering if they are a sex addict too. It can feel like an internal madness, but it is a very common and normal response.

Coping with fear and anxiety

As with anger, anxiety has physical symptoms as well as emotional. Some experience heart palpitations, difficulty catching their breath, muscle tension and a churning stomach. This is your body responding to what it perceives as a threat, and getting ready to defend itself. As with anger, living in a physical state of emergency is bad for our health, and therefore it is essential to find healthier ways to manage these feelings. Below is a three-point plan for managing anxiety and fear.

1 GET INFORMATION

The greatest of our fears are always based on the unknown, and therefore the best weapon against fear is education and information. Learning more about sex addiction will help you to know what it is that you are up against, as will joining a support group and talking to other partners. If you're concerned about sexual health, then make an appointment with your doctor

---

Sexual health fears

If your partner has been having sex with other people, then it would be wise for you to make an appointment with your local GP or sexual health clinic to be tested for STIs (sexually transmitted infections). Although you don't have to explain why you want to be tested, it can be a very difficult experience for partners. But as emotionally painful as it may be, it is much better to know that you personally do not have any health concerns resulting from your partner's sexual behaviour.

---

or local sexual health clinic, and if you're concerned about your rights if you were to divorce then make an appointment to see a solicitor.

There is one exception to the rule that information can help to reduce fears, and that is when that information includes graphic details of acting out behaviours. There are many details that can do more harm than good. See 'How facts can hurt you more' at the end of this chapter.

A false sense of urgency can often fuel our fears, leaving us feeling that we must know everything today and make decisions before it is too late. But this almost always is not true. The decisions that your fear may be driving you to make are not urgent, and rushing is likely to leave you feeling more vulnerable, not less. Take your time and be kind to yourself. Nothing is going to happen today that you can't manage, and there is plenty of time to find out what you need for the future. There is more on this at the end of this chapter.

2 BE MINDFUL

Mindfulness can be a particularly effective tool for managing anxiety. Not only is it a method that can help you to physically relax, but it also helps you to take control of your thoughts. Anxiety is created and exacerbated when we worry about the unknown or let ourselves get carried away by 'what ifs'. Learning mindfulness can help you to notice when your thoughts are taking you to negative places and can empower you to bring them back to the here and now, focusing on what's happening in the present rather than the past or the future. There are many mindfulness classes springing up around the country or you could read one of the books recommended in the further reading section at the end of this book.

3 SWITCH TO POSITIVE SELF-TALK

Having a list of positive self-affirmations can be a simple yet powerful way of combating fear and anxiety – statements such as 'I am OK', 'I am safe', 'I have people who love and support me', 'I can look after myself', 'I am surviving'. There are websites that list affirmations which can be used as a resource to find the statements that will work for you. Write down the ones that resonate with you and keep them handy so you can pull them out and recite them when you are feeling fearful or anxious. In Chapter 6 you will also find Pillars for Partners, which can also be a useful way of developing positive self-talk.

Shame

They say that shame is to addiction what oxygen is to fire. But it's not just the addict who feels great shame. More so than any other addiction, sex addiction is loaded with morality. Hence on top of the shame of dependency there is often huge shame at the acting out behaviours and the betrayal. In the survey, 92 per cent of partners said they felt shame, with 47 per cent saying it was 'extreme', 39 per cent, 'moderate' and 23 per cent, 'mild'. Shame can be particularly acute for male partners who may feel that their masculinity has been violated and may fear the harsh moral judgement that's often targeted at female sex addicts.

As previously discussed, most sex addicts are really, really nice people – loving parents, devoted partners and pillars of the community – all of which means they have further to fall from grace. Partners also experience this fall. Embarrassment, humiliation and self-doubt are common in partners who wonder how they could have lived with a sex addict and not known. 'Am I stupid?', 'Am I weak?', 'Am I responsible?' are questions that keep many partners awake at night.

Shame is fuelled by fears of what other people will think of them when, or if, they discover the truth. Many partners also feel shame at their own inability to manage emotions better, especially when they can see the impact it is having on their children. They may feel shame about the fact that they still love their spouse, in spite of what they have done to them. Indeed, there is an irony in relationships that when the person we love the most hurts us, it is to them we want to turn to most for comfort and support.

Overcoming shame

Shame thrives in isolation. This is why group work is such an essential component of addiction recovery because it provides a group of people who either say, or reflect back, the fact that 'you're OK'. The same is true for partners. Sex addiction can affect anyone and you have no reason to feel any shame or embarrassment that it has happened to you and your relationship. There is nothing you could have done to avoid this; it is absolutely no reflection on you at all. If that hasn't helped you to feel better about yourself then talk to your friends, family, professionals and, most importantly, other partners. Share your fears and vulnerabilities and believe them when they say 'you're OK', and when you're talking to other partners, notice that they are intelligent, caring and 'normal' people just like you. It is often only when you are sitting face to face with someone else in your predicament that you can truly believe 'this wasn't my fault, this had nothing to do with me'. One partner advised 'look out for you – it's not your fault'. Another said, 'there are others in the same situation. Talk and be honest on good days and bad. Look after yourself, no matter how selfishly'.

Disgust

Most partners feel some twinges of disgust (92 per cent) when they discover the extent of their partner's acting out, but for some the repulsion is sickening; 58 per cent said they felt 'extreme' disgust. Different acting out behaviours illicit different responses in partners. In part this may be due to your own personal tastes and experience, but it can also be influenced by the degree of shock you experience at the style of your partner's acting out. Some fetish behaviours can be particularly difficult to understand and you may find yourself experiencing a very visceral response. These reactions are likely to be more severe if you have personally witnessed the behaviours being acted out or seen images of it.

Escaping feelings of disgust

In some ways, overcoming disgust is easy or, at least, it's easy to say, but often much harder to do. Distraction is the best way to reduce feelings of disgust, and removing yourself from the stimuli. Human survival relies on our natural instinct to recoil and turn away from things that revolt us, and this is precisely the strategy you need to employ. If an image comes into your mind, or a thought about a behaviour, you need to think about something else, something positive and pleasurable. You may find it helpful to have something to hand, to take your mind off it – a picture of one of your children or a cute animal or a beautiful location. Or you could use a mindfulness practice such as meditation or visualisation to get yourself into a happier place. It will take practice for these techniques to work, but the golden rule is to keep at it until the disturbing image has been replaced with something pleasurable.

Relief

Last, and by no means least, a positive emotion – perhaps not positive, but at least not so painful. For 71 per cent of respondents, finding out that their partner had sex addiction brought a sense of relief. For some it felt good to know the cause of their partner's difficulties or the source of their relationship problems. For others the discovery brought to an end the constant investigation and suspicion. Some partners will have spent many years being told that their suspicions and fears were unfounded and may have even been told that it was their imagination or some fault within them. Finding out that you were right means you weren't crazy after all and your instincts were right. Some may have had a nagging anxiety that something just wasn't right, something they couldn't put their finger on, and now at last they have an explanation.

To end this section, here are some words of advice from one of the partners who completed the survey:

> Stick with it. The emotions come in waves when you least expect and are overwhelming. But the waves become less frequent and intense on the whole.

The urgent questions

In the first days and weeks after discovery or disclosure, most partners find themselves plagued by questions that demand an immediate answer. These questions usually come from wanting to seek a place of safety and stability, but time and self-care will provide that much more effectively, and often seeking answers too early can actually make the feelings of trauma worse.

In this section we are going to look at the most common immediate questions and how to manage them.

What should I do?

The answer to this question is simple, but hard to digest. Nothing except 'look after you'. Many partners want to spring into action and take positive steps, as that feels like the most productive thing to do. But few of us make wise choices and decisions when we have been through a traumatic experience. Anyone who knows about bereavement will tell you that the common advice to anyone who has lost someone close to them is to make no major decisions for at least 12 months. And as we have seen, this is a trauma that can be experienced just as acutely as any bereavement, perhaps more so.

Chapter 9 is devoted to 'can the relationship survive?'. The reason that it is so late in this book is because it is more important to look after yourself right now than to consider the future of the relationship. You deserve to take your time and give yourself the space to recover from the trauma before you begin to think about what you want and what you need. You may decide to do that while living separate from your partner for a time or, if it's a new relationship or one that was already fraught with problems, you may decide to end it immediately for those reasons. But if you don't know what you should do – do nothing. Do nothing, except take one day at a time, look after yourself and make a positive decision to decide nothing until you are fully ready.

Who should I tell?

As above, the answer to this is relatively simple. Tell no one that you may later regret telling. That will probably include children, family members and no one who you wouldn't regard as a trusted close friend who will support you. As we've already discussed, discovering that your partner has sex addiction is devastating and isolating, and all partners will benefit from having at least one person who they can talk to and confide in. That may be another partner, a therapist or someone you know.

In Chapter 10 we will explore in more depth if, how and when to tell children and other significant people, but it is important to know right now that research has shown that early disclosure to others such as children, especially when it comes from anger, is often bitterly regretted by partners (Corley and Schneider 2003). Unfortunately there are some situations where children have already found out or know that something is seriously wrong and are demanding answers themselves.

Do I know everything?

Many partners find themselves desperate for more facts and details, often to the point where they feel that seeking 'the truth' has become an all-consuming obsession. The hunt for information is a very common response and it may feel as if it's the most natural thing in the world. In the survey, 91 per cent of the respondents said they actively searched out additional details and information. But the desire for information can become a defence mechanism as all the time that your head is busy with the 'why's and your mind preoccupied with searching and seeking for truth, the pain of what you already know is avoided. But perhaps, more importantly, the facts can hurt you much, much more. A third of respondents regretted what they found out. This is what some of them said:

'I regret discovering intimate details of encounters and places encounters happened. This had a very detrimental effect on me and put visions in my head I cannot erase. It made me angrier.'

'I had too much information and therefore visualise things which may or may not happen.'

'The actual "mechanics" of what he did has created a picture in my mind that is hard to get rid of.'

'Knowing the identities and agencies of favourite prostitutes led me to do too much research into prostitution in London. Knowing the locations of meetings has ruined central London for me. I asked too many questions about what he did with them, and would prefer not to know now. I would now like to be able to wipe my memory clean.'

'A physical act – mostly on internet otherwise. Would rather not know details of act as haunts me. Harder to accept than fantasy alone.'

'Online profiles of partner and sexual preferences triggered disturbing mental images.'

Some partners will fuel their desire for more information by saying 'they have a right to know' and this is of course true, but you also have a right to protect yourself from potentially a lifetime of mental images you can't erase. Establishing the extent of your partner's behaviour is important, and may be essential for making a decision about the future of the relationship, but there are better ways of doing it and a better time. Ideally full disclosure happens within a safe therapeutic environment, which we will explore more in Chapter 11.

In reality, there is only one urgent question that partners need an answer to, and that is not found in the details of the acting out, but in their partner's recovery. That question is 'why did you do this?'. As one partner succinctly said:

In the early days I was too obsessed with details of meets. Now I have images in my head I can never erase. The details are not as important as the "why"s.

5 Understanding the cycle of reaction

If you have already read my companion book for people with addiction, *Understanding and treating sex addiction*, you'll already be aware that sex addicts get trapped in a cycle of addiction – a repeating pattern of destructive triggers, thinking and behaviours that will most likely continue until they can understand it and break it.

Once the initial shock of discovery has passed, many partners also find themselves trapped in a cycle, a repeating pattern of what often feels like an out-of-control reaction to the trauma of sex addiction. As with the cycle of addiction, there is a dormant phase, triggers, cognitive distortions, a period of regret and finally reconstitution. But the pinnacle of the cycle, as you can see in Figure 5.1, are the reactive emotions and behaviours.

Once the shock of addiction has begun to fade, many partners find themselves struggling to make sense of the endless roller coaster of destructive and out-of-control emotions, one minute feeling positive and able to cope and then, without any apparent warning, being overwhelmed by doubt, anger or despair. It's totally natural to have these emotions, and what partners seek is a sense of control and choice about what they feel, rather than drowning in destructive waves of pain. In order to do that, you need to identify where you are on the cycle, and stop it. What follows in this chapter will help you achieve that.

We'll use the example of Joanna, a solicitor in her forties, who discovered her husband's porn use and multiple infidelities with colleagues and sex workers 12 months ago.

The dormant phase

All of us are influenced by our previous life experiences. Some of those experiences will be happy ones that have helped to develop the character traits that we like about ourselves, experiences that define our values, our expectations of others and our hopes and fears for the future. Other

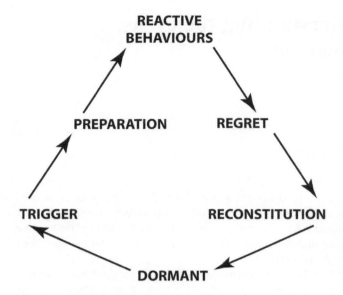

Figure 5.1 The cycle of reaction

experiences will be less happy and may have left us with scars and character traits that we don't like about ourselves.

Every partner's history is different and unique and that is why reactions can vary so greatly. When you're able to identify the key issues and events in the past, it's easier to understand how they influence the present and how they may be influencing your reaction in an unhelpful way.

For example, if you came from a family background where you witnessed the pain of infidelity in your parents' marriage then you may react to this current situation in a similar way. Or indeed, your experience may have taught you to respond in a polar opposite way. Perhaps you were brought up to be a perfectionist, to always strive for the best and not tolerate weakness in yourself or others; a family where grief and sadness wasn't shown, but instead, anger and incriminations. If this describes you then you may find it especially difficult to understand the out-of-control nature of addiction and the fallibility of your partner, and may find yourself trapped in a cycle of anger and frustration.

Previous relationships can also have a significant impact, especially if they ended in a painful or acrimonious way. When relationships come to an end it is common to wonder if you have failed in some way. For partners of sex addicts, this can compound fears and anxieties about the viability of any relationship, and leave partners feeling they are doomed to experience difficult or broken relationships.

The lifeline exercise

You can find out more about your family background and early relationships and begin to consider how it impacts your feelings today by doing what is known as a lifeline. This exercise is used in the partners' courses to help partners think about what has made them who they are today. Those who have read the book for people with addiction will notice the similarities. If you've had previous significant relationships, you can extend it to include the key moments that defined them.

First you need to get a blank sheet of paper and draw a horizontal line, as below, on which you will note the key ups and downs of your childhood from birth to present day. Positive events will be above the line, negative or painful events below. You may find the questions below helpful to get you thinking and remembering.

1 What were you told about your birth? Was it a happy event? A surprise? Or a time of difficulty?
2 How was your relationship throughout childhood with mum, dad, siblings, grandparents and any other significant people? Were there any key moments that define those relationships?
3 How was affection shown and were there any changes over the years? How was anger, discipline and conflict experienced?
4 Were there any significant losses or painful memories within the family, including such things as divorce or separation, illness or disability, parental infidelity, and moving house?
5 Were there any experiences of abuse or misuse of power/authority? Were there any times when you were made to feel ashamed or not nurtured, or betrayed?
6 How was your experience of school? How were relationships with peers and teachers at school? How did you feel about your education?
7 As you approached adolescence, what do you remember about changes in your body? What thoughts or comments did you pick up on from family and peers about relationships?
8 What memories do you have of significant emotional moments during adolescence, whether sadness, anger, conflict, pride, excitement, or boredom? Were there any significant events with friends, boyfriends or girlfriends that were difficult, or affected your self-esteem?

9 During late adolescence, what were your thoughts about who you would become in terms of your interests and aspirations relating to what you wanted from life? Career? Relationship? Children?

10 Think about early romances, sexual explorations, fumblings, first sexual experiences, first sexual intercourse. Were there any traumatic, shaming, embarrassing or particularly fantastic sexual or romantic experiences? Think about your first 'serious' relationship and any myths and messages about differences in male/female sexuality.

11 What were your personal experiences of addictions or compulsive behaviours such as chronic alcohol, drugs, over-eating or obsessive cleaning? Think about yourself, family members, friends and romantic relationships.

12 What previous romantic relationships have you had? Were they positive or negative experiences? How did they end and why?

Once you have completed this exercise you may find you can look back and see themes beginning to emerge that help you to make sense of how you're reacting now and why it may feel so difficult to move on.

Joanna's story

Joanna was the youngest of three daughters and was always teased for being the 'fat, but cute' one. She was her father's favourite and was most affected when he left their mother when her middle sister left for university. She tried very hard not to take sides, but as she was the one left at home with mum it was hard not to also feel betrayed by her father's abandonment for another woman. It had always been an affectionate and loving home, but also a very strict one where there would be frequent threats of physical punishment if the girls stepped out of line. Her middle sister was the rebellious one who dropped out of university and spiralled into a life of drug and alcohol use. Subsequently, both her sisters have gone on to have careers, get married and have children. Joanna has a good relationship with them all, although still strained with her father and his partner who he went on to marry. In later years her middle sister confided that she had been sexually abused by a neighbour's son who was 10 years older than her. Joanna also had memories of 'boundaries being crossed' with her, but it seemed her sister had much worse experiences. Joanna was bullied a bit at school for her 'puppy fat' and described herself as a late bloomer. She had a number of casual relationships and sexual partners before her first long-term boyfriend at 20 who she dated for 6 years. The relationship ended when he found out she had slept with someone else at a party, something she regretted, but realised was her way of proving she no longer wanted to be with him. She described her husband who she married 12 years ago as 'the love of her life'. They both cherished their only son who took 5 years to conceive. She thought they were very happy.

The trigger phase

One of the most frustrating experiences partners talk about is how their emotions seem to hijack them, one minute feeling as if they're managing OK and then back to square one the next. This experience is nearly always triggered by a situation or event that either consciously, or unconsciously, resurrects the painful trauma of early disclosure or discovery, such as a partner being unexpectedly late home or seeing an attractive person on the street. Or it can be triggered by something that creates an emotion associated with being the partner of an addict, for example experiencing another unrelated trauma such as a bereavement or redundancy which creates feelings of loss and anxiety. Once triggered, a partner can then find themselves spiralling down into familiar feelings of despair, rage, anxiety, depression, insecurity and/or low self-esteem. Depending on the trigger, this may be almost instantaneous, or there may be a series of triggers over a period of time that slowly drag you down.

The best way of beating this stage of the cycle is to identify and avoid triggers. For example, establishing a solid accountability contract (see Chapter 11) can help to avoid situations of insecurity within the relationship, and planning what you're going to watch on TV in advance can be helpful for avoiding triggering images or storylines, and also for establishing your boundaries, which we explore in Chapter 8.

You can use the exercise below to help you to think about the people, places, emotions, events, and routines that you already find triggering, or you think that you are most likely to find triggering. Once you have completed this, you can then look to see which triggers you can avoid, and which you need more help to manage in a more positive way. The box below were completed by Joanna.

Avoiding triggers

In the early weeks and months, at least, it is often better to avoid as many triggers as possible. So if you know that going to your local shopping centre is a place where you frequently feel triggered by other attractive shoppers or window manikins, then switch to shopping online for a while. Or you may decide that, instead of your usual summer break on the beach, you go on a walking holiday in the mountains instead. Before you switch on the television in the evening, or book to go to the cinema, or pick up a book

Recognising triggers

People	*Places*
Attractive women	Out in public anywhere with her husband
Overtly sexy women	
Her father and his partner	Crowded trains and shopping centres
'Dawn' at the office (having discovered her husband had a relationship with a woman called Dawn)	When socialising with their 'happily' married friends
	The gym and exercise classes – especially if she goes alone
Sex workers	
	The beach

Emotions	*Events and routines*
Anger	When her partner is away on business
Confusion	
	When her partner is late home
Stress	
	When travelling by public transport
Anxiety	
	Family celebrations
Feeling fat or plain	
	Anniversaries
	Storylines in some films/books/TV

to read, do some research first so you can feel more confident about the storylines.

Managing unavoidable triggers

The first thing you need to do if you find yourself triggered is to remove yourself from the source as quickly as possible and be kind to yourself. It is natural to find yourself analysing what's happened, but until you can create some distance and space for objectivity, you're more likely to make yourself feel worse. The acrostic BREATHE can be really helpful to get you away from the source of the trigger and get yourself grounded and calm again.

B **Literally breathe** – take six deep breaths, in and out. Relax your muscles, unclench your jaw, put your hand on your heart and feel the warmth of it soothing you. Allow yourself to notice how your heart rate gradually reduces to normal

R **Remove yourself from the source** – that might mean leaving a shop where someone or something has triggered you, turning off the television or quickly changing the subject.

E **Engage with your surroundings** – This can be a really useful way of getting grounded. Notice the earth beneath your feet, or the chair beneath your bottom. Look at the colours, notice the smells, listen to the sounds around you. Remember you are here now, not back there when the original trauma happened.

A **Affirm yourself** – there is more on affirmations in the next chapter, but to start you can simply say 'I am safe', 'I am OK', 'I can control my feelings', 'I will get through this'.

T **Talk to someone** – ideally phone a friend or someone who understands what you're going through, but talking to anyone can help. Start a conversation with someone at work, someone in the shop or wherever you go so you can feel connected to another human again and realise you're not alone.

H **Hang on in there** – it will take time to get over this trigger and you may have to repeat the steps above on a number of occasions before you feel calm again.

E **Encourage yourself** – you've been triggered and you've taken positive action to take control of your physical and emotional reaction. You may not manage it perfectly every time, but you are making progress and have every reason to be proud of yourself.

The preparation phase

Once you've developed positive ways of avoiding and managing triggers, you hopefully won't find yourself going into the preparation phase, but regrettably life is rarely that simple, so it is best to be prepared for the preparation phase.

This is the phase of the cycle where thoughts and behaviours can fuel the emotional state and make a negative and painful emotional reaction more likely. The most damaging thinking patterns are those that distort reality, or at least, distort the 'known' reality. In other words, thinking patterns that build from 'what if'. . . rather than facts. It is of course completely natural for partners who have been lied to and deceived to find themselves slipping into anxiety and suspicion, but attempting to ascertain the truth amid the emotion of a trigger is always counterproductive.

Below is a list of the most common unhelpful thinking patterns, or cognitive distortions as they're often referred to, that partners find themselves slipping into. You may find it useful to read through and see which ones you most often adopt.

Recognising cognitive distortions

Read the examples below and list what *you* think.

1 **Jumping to conclusions** – often there is a perfectly legitimate reason for something, but it is easy to jump to conclusions, for example when your partner is stuck in traffic or has to work late: 'he's late so he must be visiting a prostitute again' or 'he turned away from me when I was talking, so he must be looking at another woman'.

2 **Rationalisation** – this is when you make excuses for your behaviour using logic and reason. For example, 'I have to assume she/he's lying to me because they've done it so many times before', or 'it's ok to call him names as long as the children don't hear'.

3 **Justification** – when you use excuses to defend your or their behaviour. For example, 'he can't help it when he's drunk' or 'I have every right to tell his mother what he's done' or 'it's ok for me to drink too much while I'm going through this'.

4 **Minimisation** – this is a thinking strategy for not taking full responsibility for your behaviour or staying in denial. For example, 'I need to know, just this once, I must check his phone' or 'he only watched porn for 10 minutes, I guess it doesn't really count'.

5 **Magnifying** – this is the opposite of minimisation. Rather than making light of something, an event or circumstance that is relatively unimportant is given greater status. For example, 'he's been looking at his phone, which means he must be on the adult apps again and must have acted out'.

6 **Emotional reasoning** – for example, 'I'm feeling anxious, therefore s/he must have acted out' or 'I'm feeling tense and worried, therefore s/he's not telling me the truth'.

7 **Uniqueness** – this focuses on what you perceive as being unique about yourself or about your partner: 'it must be very hard for men in his position' or 'with a job like mine, I can't possibly be open and get support from others'.

8 **Victim stance** – this is when you make excuses for your partner or their behaviour by putting yourself in the role of victim. For example, 'no one can be faithful to me', 'I will never be able to survive this', or 'he can't help it, because he was abused'.

9　**Normalisation** – this is often used with generalisation to make acting out seem like 'the norm'. For example, 'all men look at pornography' or 'any partner would react like this' or 'all men lust after women in public'.

10　**Denial** – this is perhaps the most common cognitive distortion and simply involves blocking out reality. For example, 'my partner isn't acting out, he wouldn't do that again because he promised he wouldn't' or 'there is only one possible explanation for him staying up late at night to work'.

11　**Helplessness** – this can be a particularly powerful cognitive distortion, especially for those with low self-esteem. For example, 'my partner can't help himself because he's an addict' or 'I have no control over my temper because I was brought up in an angry household'.

12　**Blame** – blame is often an alternative to finding and accepting true responsibility. For example, saying 'if I was more beautiful/kinder/ sexier this wouldn't have happened', or 'if his/her mum had been more affectionate, they wouldn't have become an addict'.

In addition to negative thinking patterns, many partners also fuel their painful feeling state with unhelpful behaviours, most commonly investigating and 'scab picking'.

Investigating

In Chapter 11 we will talk more about healthy and productive ways of verifying reality and establishing accountability, and you will see that good timing is essential. If you've been triggered then the chances are that you will have lost a rational objective viewpoint and hence any kind of investigative work is more likely to make you feel worse. When coupled with cognitive distortions such as those listed above, many partners find themselves going online to check email accounts or phone records, searching the house for clues to acting out behaviours, or probing others for information. The unconscious need for these behaviours is often confusing. On the one hand it may be a strategy for seeking reassurance and stability, but it may also be a way of seeking evidence to support the negative emotion that is being experienced. For example, one partner who was triggered by seeing a very attractive redhead while out having coffee found herself overwhelmed with questions about whether or not her husband found redheads attractive. Her investigation involved going through the history of his computer to see if he had looked at redheads. Inevitably she found some, among others, so it neither confirmed her fears nor reassured her, but instead fuelled her anxiety. According to the survey, 55 per cent of respondents continued to check up on their partner, 21 per cent said 'all of the time', 46 per cent said 'frequently' and the remainder only 'occasionally' or 'rarely'.

Scab picking

We all know that picking at a scab will not only make the wound more painful, but it will also mean it takes longer to heal. Scab picking behaviours include reliving the trauma of discovery by looking back through evidence such as email exchanges or bank statements or revisiting the trauma of the acting-out behaviours such as googling massage parlours or driving round red-light districts.

Scab picking also includes behaviours that open the wounds of what was lost, for example looking at old photographs of times before the discovery, times when you thought you were happy, going through souvenirs, gifts or correspondence from the past that previously held fond memories, or putting on clothes that used to make you feel good, but now seem worthless and redundant. Many of these 'scab picking' behaviours are a natural process in loss, and there may be occasions when it is helpful to reflect on the past, but the motivation needs to be a conscious one that seeks catharsis not a triggered one that intensifies pain.

The key question that partners need to ask themselves in the preparation phase of the cycle is 'does this thinking help me feel better or worse?' and 'will doing this help me to feel better or worse?'. It is not about whether the thought or action is right or wrong, natural or strange, but whether it is helpful emotionally.

Joanna's story

Joanna knew there were times when she was her own worst enemy. The cognitive distortions she most often applied were helplessness, magnifying, generalisation and emotional reasoning. On one occasion Joanna was triggered in a restaurant by a particularly attractive young waitress that her husband joked with as he placed their order. She told herself that men just can't help themselves when there's an attractive woman around, and her feelings of insecurity proved that he didn't love her and was probably silently fantasising about the waitress. She allowed herself to spiral down into thinking about the night she'd found out, 12 months ago, and imagining that all his work in recovery was just a farce because he didn't want them to split up and not live with their son. By the time she left the restaurant she had convinced herself that the waitress thought she was fat and plain and was wondering what on earth her husband saw in her.

The reactive emotions and behaviours phase

There are many different reactive emotions and behaviours and it is important to stress that these are not necessarily wrong in themselves, but rather that they feel out of control and destructive. It is also essential to know that the emotion that feeds the behaviour is most likely completely natural and understandable, but the way it manifests is unhelpful, to everyone. The resulting behaviours are also ones that contradict a partner's sense of values and moral integrity. For example, in spite of thinking that checking up on someone behind their back is wrong, or screaming insults in a public place, they still find themselves doing it. It is the sense of personal betrayal that can be so painful. As one partner so powerfully said, 'I've become a stranger to myself'.

The most common reactive behaviours come from feelings of anger, anxiety and despair, as we explored in Chapter 4. Each of these are common responses to trauma, that is, ways of reacting when our body is thrown into fight, flight or freeze. We will look now at how these emotions can erupt.

Note that many of these behaviours are common soon after the discovery of sex addiction and are a reaction to shock and trauma. It is only when these behaviours have been continuing for longer than 4 months or so that they become part of the cycle of reaction.

Anger

Verbal attacks – many partners describe how they hear themselves shouting, swearing, insulting and threatening their partner in a way that they didn't even know they were capable of. Sometimes this may happen in public places or in front of children, who need to be protected from uncontrolled, frightening outbursts.

Physical assault – it is common in groups to hear stories of how partners have slapped, punched, kicked or thrown things in the middle of an argument or sometimes out of the blue. Physical violence is never OK. Never. Often the person with the addiction feels they deserve what they are getting, but nonetheless, it is not OK, and therapists take risks to safety very seriously. Sometimes the assault is not on the person, but to property. Again, this is never OK and not a healthy way to express anger.

Inappropriate disclosure – while some partners do not want anyone to know what's going on, others want to scream it from the rooftops, to shame the addict. Disclosure may be to strangers in a public place, to work colleagues or employers, to extended family members or to children. Disclosure may be appropriate at certain times, to some people, but it needs to be done in a controlled way. Children who find out about sex addiction from an angry parent often resent being told, and can become angry with the person who told them.

Self-harming – In the partners survey, 27 per cent had self-harmed in some way or considered it. Regrettably this is a common way of managing anger that feels as if it has no other outlet. Self-harm may take the form of deliberate self-injury such as cutting or burning, but may also be self-starvation, excessive alcohol and/or drug use or refusing to take prescription medication. As with physical violence, this is not OK and further professional help should be sought immediately.

Fear and anxiety

Panic attacks – racing heart, clammy palms, breathlessness; these are common signs of panic attacks and a common response to trauma. If you are experiencing physical symptoms of anxiety it is important to seek professional help to find a better way of dealing with the feelings rather than accepting it as an inevitability.

Hypervigilance – many partners find it impossible to relax, and may feel that they are permanently on edge, experiencing restlessness, nail-biting, constant clock-watching and scanning for people and potential threats whenever away from home. Hypervigilance can be exhausting, permanently living on a knife-edge.

Checking – checking behaviours are similar to hypervigilance but more conscious. They may include looking through emails, checking internet history or tracking software reports, or simply phoning a partner to find out what they're doing 'right now'. Unlike investigating in the preparation phase, checking is the result of being triggered, and doesn't result in another episode of explosive or damaging behaviour. The actions stop when a conclusion has been reached, such as feeling reassured that nothing has happened and there are no secrets, but it is done in a way that feels wrong, and incongruent with personal values.

Grief and despair

Withdrawal – feelings of despair often make us want to withdraw from the world for a while, but when that is happening on a regular and protracted basis, then it can become damaging. When withdrawal is part of reactive behaviours it doesn't come from a place of conscious choice, but feels more of a desperate survival strategy. Withdrawal may be emotional, not engaging with anyone; or it may be physical, not seeing anyone.

Some partners find they withdraw from work, from friends, from family, and some, from children too.

Depression – some partners may *feel* depressed, while others may *become* depressed. When it is the latter, then it is important to seek advice from your doctor, but when it is 'feelings' of depression they will pass, as the next phase of the cycle is reached. A phase of depression is often accompanied by disturbances in sleeping and eating patterns, tearfulness, malaise and lack of motivation to continue with any normal routines. This may extend into becoming withdrawn, as above.

Joanna's story

That night in the restaurant was one of Joanna's rock-bottom moments. It was her birthday and it had been her idea that they went out for a meal. As she allowed the trigger of the attractive waitress to build, she became more and more withdrawn. She became monosyllabic in every conversation her husband tried to start, and she moaned about the food and refused to eat it. But she drank copious amounts of wine. She was increasingly abrupt and rude with the waitress as she served them over the evening and Joanna finally stormed out just as the dessert arrived. She physically pushed past the waitress and glared at her venomously. Once out on the street, she realised just how drunk she was, and scrambled into a taxi, barking directions at the driver as her husband tried to get her to stop. People on the street were staring as she left the scene and, once home, she began sobbing uncontrollably. Her husband arrived home about 10 minutes later and held her hair back as she vomited down the toilet before helping her get undressed and putting her to bed.

The regret phase

Many partners find themselves bitterly regretting what they've done while overwhelmed with emotion. The regret may be because of very specific immediate consequences to self or others, or the consequences may take some time to appear. For example, sometimes it is weeks after an inappropriate disclosure that partners finds themselves desperately wishing they could take back what they've said. On other occasions it may be waking up with the 'hangover from hell' or regretting not joining in with a family occasion.

The regret phase is often accompanied by feelings of fear and shame. When partners have reacted in a way that is out of control, and often out of character, it heightens their sense that life has now spiralled out of control. Nothing feels stable and reliable anymore, not even themselves.

Joanna's story

> When Joanna woke up the morning after the restaurant incident, the memories of what had happened came flooding back, along with a thumping headache. She was mortified by her behaviour, particularly to the waitress. She had made a horribly embarrassing scene and had treated an innocent young girl terribly. She felt awful about herself. Both she and her sisters had been waitresses in their teens and knew first-hand how horrible some customers can be. One of the things she liked about her husband was how polite and friendly he always was with people in the service professions. It was a value they'd shared and, regardless of what her husband's motives might have been, she had breached it and she could not excuse herself for her behaviour.

The reconstitution phase

The reconstitution phase is the place where partners attempt to 'pull themselves together' and try to establish a sense of normality. This may include emotional and cognitive strategies, such as positive self-talk, talking to friends and generally 'putting things into perspective'. For some, this also includes productive conversations with a partner and committing to getting the relationship back on track. On the surface these are often very sensible and practical strategies, but they can serve as defence mechanisms that don't resolve deeper, historic causes of the emotional reaction.

The reconstitution phase ends when a partner returns to dormant. The waves of anger, anxiety and shame have passed, or at least subsided. It may feel calmer and more stable again and, depending on how long you stay in dormant, it may finally feel as if you're 'coping'. But the nature of cycles is that unless you've found the brakes, you will go round again. And therefore it's just a matter of time before another trigger or series of triggers throws you into the emotional maelstrom again.

Joanna's story

> Joanna and her husband talked through what had happened the night before, and they were quickly able to get back onto an even keel. He was angry with her for her behaviour, but knew her well enough to know it was completely out of character and that she was genuinely wracked with guilt. Joanna soothed herself by saying she was going through an extremely emotional time and vowed not to go back to that restaurant again. But she also realised that she had to learn more productive ways of handling triggers and also had to take time to look at her issues of low self-esteem that went

back to her childhood and explore how her experiences of childhood abuse and her parents' divorce were fuelling her reactions.

Breaking the cycle of reaction

Breaking the cycle will take time and effort, but it is something that all partners must do in order to regain a sense of stability and find a safe place from which to make decisions for the future.

For some people, identifying the phases with the exercises above and using the tools to manage triggers, and the strategies in Chapter 4 to manage difficult emotions will suffice. But many benefit from additional professional help to work through the stories of their past and take control of their emotional responses. The support of other partners can also provide an essential resource for breaking through feelings of isolation and giving practical advice and encouragement. You can find more information on professional services, and further reading, at the end of this book.

6 Repairing self-identity and self-esteem

What kind of person lives, knowingly or unknowingly, with someone with sex or porn addiction? What kind of person has no idea that the person closest to them is leading a double life? What kind of person is rejected sexually in favour of porn or sex workers? What kind of person loves someone who has hurt and betrayed them so much? These are the questions that keep partners of sex addicts awake at night. Not just 'how could they . . .?', but 'how could I . . .?'. But as one partner who completed the survey said, 'This is your partner's issue, NOT yours, it doesn't define who YOU are'.

Perhaps the most damaging impact of sex addiction is what it does to a partner's sense of self-identity and self-worth. While rationally you may know that you are not to blame and that you did not 'cause' it, nonetheless, knowing you've lived with it can be devastating emotionally and spiritually. Sex addiction can also have a profound impact on a partner's sexuality, which we will explore in depth in Chapter 12. Partners of sex addicts can find themselves doubting their very sense of self – not just their self-esteem that tells them what they're worth, but their self-identity that defines who they are. In this chapter we will look at repairing both.

Who am I?

Our self-identity is complex and multi-layered. At its simplest, it defines our basic human characteristics, perhaps including our gender, ethnicity and age. Hence I would describe myself as a 49-year-old white woman. For many, it also includes their primary occupation and, for some, their sexual orientation. So I might add that I'm heterosexual and a psychotherapist. If you have a strong faith or political views, you might also add that you are a Christian, a feminist or a labour supporter (or indeed all the above!). The words we choose are strongly influenced by our societal context and our current life stage. Hence being Jewish, or an eldest son, pregnant, or a graduate will be top of the list for some.

In all cultures, we tend to identify ourselves by the things that we value most, the things that we feel most define us, which means that part of that definition includes our primary relationships with others, such as being a wife and a mother. It might also include other activities that you engage in on a regular basis. The exercise below can help you to think about your self-identity.

Take a sheet of paper and a pen and draw a circle in the middle to represent the centre of a flower and put your name in it. Now draw petals around the edge, with the names of all the relationships and roles that you have, gradually building up your flower as you think of more and more. Below is an example of one that Alice drew.

Once you've completed this exercise, hopefully you'll be able to see just how many things there are in your life that make you the person that you are, more than just a partner of someone with sex addiction, but someone with many different roles and relationships. Keep this picture handy as you can use it again as we go on to think about self-esteem. But first we'll look at another key component of self-identity.

Figure 6.1 Alice's flower

Values

Who we are is influenced heavily by what we believe, by the value system that we hold dear. Sex addiction not only compromises the value system of those who suffer from it, but also those who love them. Many partners find themselves reacting in ways that are not in line with their personal value system. They may find themselves saying and doing things that they would never normally do, things that they fundamentally believe are wrong; things that leave them feeling ashamed and morally compromised.

Values can be broken down into two distinct categories. There are the universal values such as being honest, caring, reliable and non-judgemental, and there are practical values that relate to our individual circumstances, such as the principles you hold most dear about how to treat your family and friends, how to manage your money and look after your home and how to look after yourself. Our values are the things that give our life a sense of meaning, purpose and fulfilment. When we live in line with our values we feel good about ourselves and we are able to make decisions and set priorities.

There are, of course, times when our values seem to contradict each other, and this can be particularly true in the aftermath of discovering sex addiction. It can be tempting to throw your own values out of the window if your partner seems to have done so. But reclaiming those values is an essential part of rebuilding your own self-identity – taking back what is yours and living in a way that you value.

What am I worth?

Self-esteem is a term that encompasses both self-confidence and self-worth. In other words, it describes how we feel about our character, our strengths and our skills. Our sense of self-worth starts early in childhood. If you were brought up being told you were a clever, beautiful, resourceful, kind, loving and friendly little human being then you are likely to have positive self-esteem. But if you received negative messages, then you may have a different view. Our self-esteem is also affected by our relationships with friends and previous primary relationships. If you were treated with care and respect, then you're more likely to believe that is what you deserve, but if you've been treated badly then your sense of self-worth may be low. Life experiences also have an impact. Things such as career problems, issues with close friends or family, infertility, or financial difficulties can all affect how we feel about ourselves. If you were someone who struggled with low self-esteem in the past, then low self-esteem may be a particularly big issue for you now.

Whatever your current level of self-esteem, the following exercise will help you to think more deeply about your positive attributes and strengths.

Take your self-identity flower, and, next to each petal, write down a few words to describe the qualities that you bring to each of those roles. If you're struggling, think about what others would say about you – or call them and ask them! Don't worry if you're repeating some of the same words. This just demonstrates how important that attribute of yours is to other people. Below is an example of how Alice completed hers.

If you're finding it difficult to complete this exercise then there's an excellent online tool at www.authentichappiness.sas.upen.edu where you can answer a brief questionnaire that will help you to think about which of the twenty-four identified strengths are your top ones, or your 'signature strengths' as Martin Seligman, author of *Authentic happiness* calls them (Seligman 2003).The twenty-four strengths are broken down under six headings, and identifying your strengths can not only help to boost your self-esteem, but can also help you to face your future with confidence.

- **Wisdom and knowledge** – creativity, curiosity, judgement, love of learning, perspective

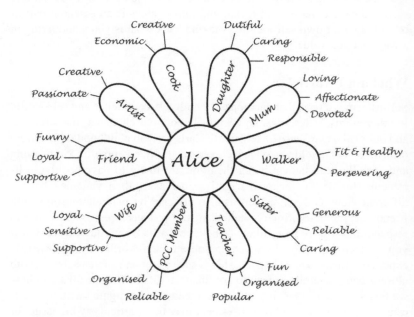

Figure 6.2 Flower with words

- **Courage** – bravery, perseverance, honesty, zest
- **Humanity** – love, kindness, social intelligence
- **Justice** – teamwork, fairness, leadership
- **Temperance** – forgiveness, humility, prudence, self-regulation
- **Transcendence** – appreciation of beauty and excellence, gratitude, hope, humour, spirituality.

Strengthening self-identity

There is a metaphor that I find helpful when thinking about strengthening self-identity. Imagine in your mind a building that is held up by a series of pillars. That building is your life, and each of the pillars represents a core part of your identity. One of those pillars, i.e. your relationship, is crumbling – or it may have completely collapsed, but the other pillars are still there. The structure of your building may be weaker at the moment, but if you put up some scaffolding where the relationship pillar stands, then it will not collapse. That scaffolding consists of the emotional coping strategies that we explored in Chapter 4 and the tools you use to manage triggers that we looked at in Chapter 5 – the strategies that you will use to help you survive the trauma and manage the roller coaster of emotions. These are temporary measures that will support your life over the coming months until either your relationship pillar is rebuilt, or is replaced by something else.

In the meantime, you can focus your physical and emotional energy on the other pillars that support you. That might be your relationship with your children and/or your friends. It might be your career and/or a hobby or pastime that has particular significance for you. There can be a temptation in desperate times to withdraw from other relationships and activities, and to some extent that is not a bad idea as you need to preserve your resources. But don't let yourself withdraw from the things that can help to keep your sense of identity grounded, places where you know who you are and what your role is.

Boosting self-esteem

There are many excellent books written on boosting self-esteem, some of which you will find in the further reading section at the end of this book, but, for now, here are a few practical ideas.

Be physically healthy

'Healthy body, healthy mind' is a well-known cliché that we increasingly accept as truth. When our body is strong we are more resilient to physical and emotional stress. We are more able to fight off viruses and infections and we have more energy to focus on our emotional needs. Our physical health can be optimised by paying attention to the following three areas:

1   **Sleep** – it is well known that sleep is essential for our physical health and wellbeing and it is recommended that adults get 8 hours' sleep per night. If you're struggling to sleep, establish a good relaxing bedtime routine and try one of the many natural insomnia remedies that are now available.

2   **Exercise** – when we exercise, we automatically trigger our natural feel-good chemicals, whether that's running, going to the gym, playing competitive sports or something more sedate such as Pilates or t'ai chi. Exercise can help relieve stress and reduce depression.

3   **Diet** – in addition to maintaining a healthy diet of sufficient calorific intake and an appropriate balance of proteins, complex carbohydrates and fresh fruit and vegetables, some supplements are thought to be particularly beneficial for helping with stress, lemon balm, valerian, 5-HTP and St John's wort, to name a few. If you want to explore this route, a reputable dietician will be able to help you further.

Spend time with friends

Socialising may be the last thing you feel like doing right now, but being with other people can not only be a great source of support, but can also add perspective and provide a much-needed break from the pain of being the partner of a sex addict. There are two very different types of friendships that can support you in different ways. For example:

•   **Close friends** – this is the person, or if you're lucky, a few people who you feel closest to. You may have known them for a long time and you may see them often, but not necessarily. Closeness and contact are not the same thing; what defines a close friend is how quickly you can fall into step with them, even when the absences have been long. A close friend is someone you can be honest with who you know won't judge you, even though they may challenge you if they feel it's in your best interests. They're someone who you can rely on to listen and support you, someone you can both laugh and cry with.

•   **Functional friends** – these friends are people that play a particular role in your life. You will like each other, but probably not describe yourselves as close. You share a common interest such as a hobby, being parents together or working in the same place. These are the people you can chat to, who won't ask personal or intimate questions. These are recreational relationships, and a functional friend can be particularly beneficial when you need a social buddy to help you get lost in another activity and lift your mood.

Many partners struggle to tell anyone about what they are going through because they are so afraid of the judgement both they, and their partner, may receive. This is particularly true for male partners who may additionally fear that their friends may doubt their masculinity or be lasciviously intrigued by the details of their partner's acting out. If you genuinely feel there is no one within your current circle of friends that you can confide in, then there are online forums for partners where you can get support. Or find out if there is a partner group in your area where you can receive professional help as well as the mutual support of people who know what you're going through.

Have fun

This may seem like a crazy suggestion, but laughter really is a powerful medicine. Many partners feel as though they have been robbed of their sense of joy and fun. They often feel as if they've been thrown into a permanent parent-like role where they are forced to be the responsible one in the relationship, constantly alert to possible dangers, and fluctuating between nurturing their partner's recovery and policing it. There is more on how to avoid this in Chapter 8 and Chapter 11.

You may not feel like having fun with your partner right now, but hopefully you can find friends with whom you can 'play', people who will allow you to enjoy the child-like elements of your personality such as being creative, spontaneous and even silly! If you have children, they are an excellent resource for getting in touch with our fun side and they'll love it too. If you don't have children, then make time for yourself to watch a comedy on the television, rent a funny film or read something amusing. YouTube is full of funny moments that can give you a break from the serious solemnity of being a partner of a sex addict.

Develop positive self-talk

Everyone has a voice in their head that tells them who they are. If that voice is telling you that you've been stupid, or naïve, or unlovable or that you'll never be happy again, then tell it to shut up. That voice is you, and it's yours to control, so whenever you're tempted to say something bad about yourself, stop and replace it with something positive. If it helps, write a list of positive affirmations, such as you're beautiful, you're lovable, you will get through this, you will be happy again and enjoy life. It can be difficult to change that voice, especially if it is one that has been around for years, but it can be done, and you deserve it.

In addition to changing your self-talk, you may also find it helpful to adopt what is known as the pillars. Similar to the building we talked about earlier, these positive paragraphs can be a useful way of rebuilding the structure of your life.

The principle of pillars is that they can be used to prop you up when you feel as if you are falling apart. They can be used to remind you that you do have control over your life, to remind you that you can and will survive. There are pillars for addicts to use that remind them that they can change and are changing, the pillars for partners are similar in as much as they are designed to be a reminder to partners that they are strong, independent individuals who are getting stronger.

The original idea for the pillars came from Dr Matthew Hedelius and Dr Todd Freestone from the Comprehensive Treatment Clinic in the US, and the recommendation is that the pillars are read out loud, three times a day for a month, starting with pillar 1 and then working through to pillar 5. As you repeat the words to yourself over and over again, you will find that your thinking begins to change. Some partners have preferred to read each for a week at a time and then repeat over a period of months. Experiment with what works for you.

PILLAR 1 – I AM RESPONSIBLE FOR ME

I am responsible for me. I am responsible for my feelings and for my behaviours. I did not cause my partner's sex addiction and I did not ask for this to happen, but I will survive this. I will take each day at a time and I will endeavour to manage my feelings in a healthy way that makes me feel stronger and proud to be me. As each day passes, I am learning more about myself and I am getting stronger.

PILLAR 2 – I CANNOT CHANGE MY PARTNER

I cannot change my partner's behaviour, nor can I control it. Things may happen that make me feel hurt and angry, and when that happens I will manage it in a healthy way. The nature of addiction is that sometimes there may be lapses and relapses and I cannot control that. I am responsible for setting my boundaries and making my needs known. I have a right to share how I feel, but I cannot control what another human being does. Acknowledging that I cannot change my partner can make me feel empowered and grow stronger.

PILLAR 3 – I CHOOSE WHAT I THINK

I choose how I think, I can focus on pain and sadness or I can focus on the things that I enjoy and value in life. I have friends and family who love me and I can think about them when I feel alone. When I have intrusive thoughts, I can choose whether or not I ruminate on them or whether I choose to think about something else. I can choose what I think about, and choosing positive things will help me to grow stronger.

PILLAR 4 – I CHOOSE HOW I SPEND MY TIME

I can choose how I spend my time. Before I found out about the addiction I had many different things in my life. I am more than just a partner of a sex addict, I have other relationships and other activities that are meaningful to me. I can choose to spend more of my time doing things that I enjoy, things that make me feel positive about myself and things that give my life meaning. I will choose how to spend my time in a way that makes me grow stronger.

PILLAR 5 – MY FUTURE

No one is fully in control of their future, but I can make plans to enjoy a life that is not controlled by my partner's addiction. My relationship may not survive this addiction, but I can. My thoughts and my behaviours are within my control and I am in control of my hopes and dreams for the future. It is up to me to decide how I want to live my life and how to live a life that is in line with my values and the future that I desire. As I grow stronger, I am reaching for the future that I desire.

Practise good self-care

In *Your sexually addicted spouse*, Barbara Steffens and Marsha Means stress the importance of incorporating good self-care activities into each day and talk about how this can help to manage the burden of stress that comes with being the partner of a sex addict. In addition to some of the ideas already covered in this chapter, they also talk about maintaining as many usual routines as possible, saying 'no' to people when you need or want to and giving yourself a break and not expecting too much from yourself.

Finally, many partners have also found that the Three Cs that were popularised by Al Anon for the families of alcoholics are a useful regular mantra to ensure the focus remains on self-care, rather than their partner's behaviour. The Three Cs are:

You didn't **C**ause it – you can't **C**ontrol it – and, you can't **C**ure it.

7 Facing the future

In the last chapter we looked at how being a partner of a sex addict doesn't determine a partner's identity and self-worth, and in this chapter we'll explore how being a partner doesn't have to determine the future. There will be practical tools for identifying and achieving areas for growth and change, and suggestions for places to go for additional support and help. But all of that will be wasted unless the pain of addiction can be left behind. So this chapter will end on the touchy topic of forgiveness.

Most of us have a rough idea of what we want in life and in which direction we're heading. But in reality, these assumptions of our future are always fragile. The news is full of stories of people whose lives are changed in a fraction of a second as a result of illness, accident, crime or someone else's failing. The truth is that we never know what the future holds and all we can do is base our hopes and plans on where we stand today.

All partners find themselves facing a different future to the one they thought. For some, that future may mean separating from the relationship, which we will explore more in Chapter 9, but, for all, it will be a future that is no longer based on the solid foundation of a relationship. This may sound like a very negative and depressing statement, but it could be argued that basing your life on another is never truly a solid foundation. No one can be sure of the course of their relationship, hence exploring other areas of life that give meaning and fulfilment is a wise decision. For partners of sex addicts, it is especially important to embrace, and invest in, every area of life and develop a balanced lifestyle – a lifestyle that is not dependent on the quality of a relationship. As we've talked about before, in the first 6 months after discovering addiction, the priority is simply to survive the trauma and understand the cycle of reaction. But with that achieved, now is the time to look at the future.

Developing a balanced lifestyle

Back in Chapter 6 we explored the importance of reclaiming your values and how these form the basis of our identity. Those values are also key in determining our priorities in life and the way that we find a sense of meaning and purpose in the things that we do. There are a number of different opinions on what constitutes a balanced life, but most agree that it is a combination of work, rest and play – sometimes alone, sometimes with others. In my experience, a balanced life includes eight elements: relationship, friendship, family, fun, relaxation, personal growth, work and social contribution. The importance of each of these areas will vary from individual to individual and change over the course of life. To maintain balance, we must be ready to adapt when circumstances dictate, but no element should be entirely absent. We will now explore what each of these areas of life means in more depth:

1 **Relationship** – This refers to a primary couple relationship. A stable couple relationship is an important part of many people's lives, but regrettably it is always compromised, if not completely shattered, by sex addiction. If you have already worked through the shock of discovery or disclosure, your partner is in recovery and you've decided to stay, then you may be ready to think about your relationship and whether or not you want to work on it. But if not, this may be an area to leave at the moment. For those who are single, the relationship area of life would best describe the most significant friendship – the person who you feel closest to and has most influence in your life.

2 **Friends** – A friend in need is a friend indeed – or so the saying goes, and when you've discovered sex addiction, it's a time when friends can play an especially important role, whether that is close friends or functional friends as we explored in the last chapter.

3 **Family** – Nowadays, families come in many different shapes and sizes. Parents, step-parents, grandparents, step-grandparents, siblings, half-siblings, step-siblings, aunts, uncles, cousins, nieces, nephews and a whole load of other second or in-law relations. There might also be other family friends who play, or have played, a significant role in family life and, of course, children of whatever age. A crisis such as discovering sex addiction will bring some family members closer, and leave others further away. Family relationships vary considerably between different cultures, and each of us has a different expectation of how a family 'should' operate. The discovery, or disclosure, of addiction may high-light problems that have been around for many years, or may reveal a depth of understanding and support that had hitherto gone unnoticed or

been taken for granted. Either way, family in whatever way you define it, or experience it, is an inevitable part of life that can be maximised for optimum reward.

4 **Fun and recreation** – Play is part of being human. From birth to old age, the desire to have fun, to laugh and be creative, is universal. In terms of transactional analysis, this area of life emanates from the free child. The pain of discovering addiction often robs people of their ability to get in touch with their inner free child, and innocent fun may be a dim and distant memory. Getting back in touch with this part of ourselves and giving it a place to express itself in our lifestyle is a key component of becoming whole and healthy again. In order to reintroduce fun, some people find it helpful to think back to activities that used to be enjoyed before the addiction took grip, or to remember the things that you were always going to do 'one day'. This is where group work can often be beneficial, as others share the things they enjoy and members can encourage each other to have fun again. There are an endless list of things that might be classed as fun and recreational, but broadly speaking they will be pursuits that include some element of physical or mental energy, such as sport or physical exercise, a creative hobby, travelling or visiting places, further education, competitive games, DIY, gardening, laughing with friends, cooking, wine-making, bee-keeping, playing an instrument, singing and so on.

5 **Rest and relaxation** – Many activities that might be classed as fun and recreational are not necessarily relaxing. While it is important to have activities that stimulate us, it's also important to have periods of time that are devoted to slowing down. Busyness seems to be a curse of twenty-first-century living and many people feel guilty if they're not doing something perceived as productive with their time. But relaxing is productive, because it allows us to recharge our batteries and gives space for inspiration to be born. Many partners find themselves caught in a state of almost constant high arousal and hence it is even more important to find ways to relax. As with fun and recreation, some people find it easier to relax in the company of other people while others prefer to be alone. Either is fine as long as both the body and mind are able to be relaxed. For some, relaxation has a spiritual quality and is best enjoyed in religious practices or in communion with nature. Other typical activities might include reading, listening to music, gentle exercise, meditation, watching TV or films, playing chess, enjoying scenery and so on.

6 **Work** – Another area of our lives that can give satisfaction is work. That could be voluntary work, paid employment, part-time or full-time. Whatever form work takes, it is a place where you have the potential

to feel good about what you give and produce and what you receive in terms of financial and/or emotional reward. If work is not a source of reward then it may be time for a career change, but if that's not possible, expanding in other areas of life can make an unsatisfactory job more tolerable.

7 **Personal growth** – Where work is not a source of pleasure, it is especially important to take time to focus on personal growth. It is the nature of being human that we enjoy learning. We like to expand our knowledge and our skill set and to feel a sense of achievement that comes from personal endeavour. Since this is an area of life that is not dependent on other people, it provides an opportunity to be completely focused on personal needs and desires. Some will be fortunate enough to gain personal growth from their employment, but, since most jobs require working on behalf of the team or the company, an additional element of self-focused growth can be beneficial. Personal growth means different things to different people. It may be learning a new skill such as a language or playing an instrument, or a new craft such as painting or carpentry. Or it might mean emotional growth through therapy, reading or mindfulness exercises, or spiritual growth through prayer, mediation and other religious practices. It doesn't matter what it is as long as there is a sense of self-improvement and progress.

8 **Contribution** – Contribution is perhaps the opposite of personal growth. It refers to the part of life where we give to others or give back to society. It is the place where we can develop our empathy and enjoy the rewards of altruism. When we give to others, it also allows us step outside of ourselves and see the world from another perspective. Depending on the activity, it can also provide a positive sense of agency and influence. Making a contribution may mean getting more involved in a political party, either as a supporter or a candidate, or maybe a social issue such as poverty, housing, immigration, children and young people's welfare, physical or mental health, the elderly, education or public services. Or it may mean perhaps helping a charity that specialises in environmental projects, working in the third world, fighting for human rights or animal welfare. Some partners of recovering addicts, especially those in 12-step communities, choose to give back in some way to support fellow partners of addiction sufferers.

These eight areas of life are not in order of importance and it may be that one area, such as relationships or employment is at times completely missing. If that is the case then other areas can be focused on to ensure that life is still experienced as fulfilling. In fact, it is often when one of these key areas is taken away, as so often happens as a result of sex addiction, that the

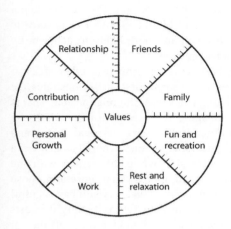

Figure 7.1 Life wheel

importance of the other areas of life becomes apparent. Unfortunately it is not always possible to have a balanced life, but we can endeavour to do so.

In Figure 7.1 you will see an image of a life wheel. This is a concept widely used in life coaching as a tool to discover which areas of life may need more attention. The principle is that by looking at the wheel and marking your degree of satisfaction between 1 and 10 on each axis, you can see how balanced your life is and therefore how smoothly the wheel of life will turn. The higher the marks you are able to score yourself, the richer your life will be and the more overall satisfaction you are likely to gain from it. Completing the life wheel can provide valuable information about the areas of life where change is both desired and required. As you can see from the diagram, all of these eight areas of life should come from a central point of your value system.

Once you have completed the life wheel exercise you should be able to identify areas where you would like to grow and change. Whether or not your relationship is going to survive the addiction, joy and fulfilment can be gained from other areas of life if and when you are ready to work on them. One of the most effective ways of both committing to change and monitoring progress is to set what are known as SMART goals.

Setting SMART goals

Like most people, you will almost certainly have set yourself goals and targets at some time in your life but, like most, you have probably not achieved all of them. One of the most common reasons that people do not achieve their goals is because they are not SMART. SMART is an acrostic that can help you to write goals that you are more likely to achieve, by ensuring they are both practical and achievable.

For partners of sex addicts, setting goals for growth in other areas of their life is beneficial for a number of reasons. First, it demonstrates the fact that there is more to life than being in a successful relationship. That is not to minimise how painfully damaging the betrayal of sex addiction is, but it improves quality of life in friendships, work, personal growth and so increases confidence that life does still go on. Second, it can be a productive distraction from the relationship while the person with the addiction gets themself into recovery. Third, it provides a sense of purpose and agency, allowing partners to feel empowered that they still have control of their lives and can make decisions about their future. Finally it boosts self-esteem, not only in achieving the goals but in ticking them off the list as achieved.

The acrostic SMART can be used for any size of goal, and stands for:

S   **Specific** – To achieve a goal it needs to be specific. In other words, you need to know exactly what it is that you are aiming for. For example, 'relax more' is not specific, whereas 'read' is.

M   **Measurable** – Quantifying your goal will also improve your chances of reaching it. For example, rather than just saying 'read', say 'read one chapter a week'.

A   **Achievable** – Many goals fail because they are set too high. It is much better to set it low and then extend it than risk failing. Hence reading one chapter of a book a week is probably achievable, whereas reading a whole book is not.

R   **Relevant and realistic** – If your goal is to improve your relaxation, then the activity you choose has got to be relevant to relaxation, hence reading a work book may not be SMART. It also needs to be realistic in terms of the resources you have and your personality. If you don't like reading, then it's not a realistic goal.

T   **Time-related** – Setting a specific timescale for your goals can help to keep motivation going to achieve them as you tick them off. So to make your relaxation goal fully SMART it would be 'read one chapter of a novel each week until the end of the year'.

Below are examples of other SMART goals that partners have set:

•   See friends for one evening every month starting next month.
•   Start piano lessons before the end of March.

- Go to Pilates at least three times each month starting next week.
- Take the children to Legoland during the school summer holidays.
- Google local environmental projects that recruit volunteers, before the end of April.
- Telephone or write to Mandy (friend who moved away) and arrange to meet up before the end of March.
- Spend at least 15 minutes a day in the garden.

As you can see, setting SMART goals can help to keep focused on what you want to achieve and give you a sense of progress and growth as you achieve it. One partner wisely gave this advice:

> You can't control your partner's addiction/behaviours/lying or whatever. Invest in yourself, your career/friends/hobbies/independence, whatever is important in your life, so that you have a route out of the relationship if or when you want or need to leave.

Finding forgiveness

Whatever decision you make for your future and for your relationship, forgiveness is essential for recovering and moving forward. All the time you hold on to bitterness and resentment over what has happened, you continue to lock yourself into the past, weighted down with pain and anger. When you forgive, you free yourself from painful emotions and give yourself the chance to live again.

Some people struggle with the word forgiveness because it has religious connotations and is often confused with 'forgetting', 'letting someone off the hook' or saying that what happened 'doesn't matter anymore'. But forgiveness is psychologically essential and one of the most powerful tools for healing the human heart. Forgiving someone doesn't mean you're condoning their behaviour or saying that you're willing to tolerate it. And it certainly doesn't mean that you've given the offender a pardon – the price must still be paid. Crucially it does not mean that you want to be reconciled or that the relationship will work. It is quite possible to forgive your partner but still choose to separate. Some partners maintain a misconception that not forgiving will in some way protect them from future pain or the risk of their partner relapsing, but, regrettably, that is not the case.

First and foremost, forgiveness is a conscious choice to let go of pain. It is a process, not a single event, and it takes time and a huge amount of effort. Most partners find it easier to forgive in small chunks. Rather than trying to forgive what's happened, it may be easier to start with letting go of some of the acting-out behaviours such as pornography use, or some of the lies. Or you may find it easier to start with forgiving that your partner didn't recognise it as sex addiction and seek help sooner, perhaps because little help or information was available. Or you may forgive that they are an addict, but need more time to forgive the consequences.

Blocks to forgiveness

- **Wanting justice** – sex addiction isn't fair, and partners rightfully feel that they are the innocent victims. Feeling angry and wanting justice, and perhaps also wanting to punish by constantly reminding them of what they've done is understandable. But no one can change the past, and whatever you do doesn't change the fact that you were treated unfairly. Forgiving is your opportunity to leave your painful feelings in the past and seek justice in the future. Not allowing yourself to do that is an even greater injustice.
- **Wanting control** – some partners will hold on to the pain of the past in an attempt to control their partner's future choices. By continuing to demonstrate their hurt and anger they hope to maintain their partner's undivided attention and compliance and the right to speak about the issues at any time. Forgiving doesn't mean that the pain is over and can be forgotten, but it does facilitate reduction in painful feelings and allow the space for conversations and decisions to be based on rational choice rather than emotional manipulation.
- **Wanting safety** – withholding forgiveness can give a false sense of safety and security. Some partners fear that if they forgive their partner then they may forget the pain they've caused and do it again. But, in reality, not forgiving just fuels your insecurity and means that damaged emotions never get the chance to heal. By forgiving, you become strong again and have more energy and motivation to focus on either ending the relationship or building one with boundaries and accountability (more in Chapters 8 and 11).

Ultimately it is much easier to forgive if the offender is sorry and demonstrates true remorse. We will talk about this further in Chapter 11 where we talk about rebuilding trust. If your partner has not taken responsibility for their addiction or their recovery, or even acknowledged their addiction, then forgiveness may be a one-sided process. It may mean that reconciliation is impossible but, nonetheless, forgiveness can free you from the gaping wounds of pain and allow them to heal.

Finding further help

Some partners are reluctant to reach out for help, with some saying that it is 'the addict's problem, not theirs' and hence the addicts are the ones that need help, not them. A colleague aptly likened this to someone who has been run over by a bus refusing to go to Accident & Emergency because they weren't the one who was driving!

But partners find it hugely beneficial to reach out to others for both peer and professional support. Being a partner of a sex addict can be extremely isolating and leaves many partners dogged with self-doubt and fears for the future. Professional counselling, whether alone or within a group environment can provide a springboard for personal growth as a deeper understanding of self is gained and a greater awareness of the strengths and skills required to move positively into the future. Support from other partners can also be invaluable for breaking through negative feelings and providing hope of better things to come. In the survey I asked what advice partners would give others in their situation. This is just a sample of those who, in one way or another, said 'seek help' – there were many more:

'I would advise anyone going through this to seek advice and support. There are many partners going through the same thing. Take care of your health, mentally and emotionally, and talk to people who you can trust. Don't do it alone.'

'Get help! I thought I could help him myself and it turned out not to be the case. There is professional help available, don't be ashamed to ask. I did not talk to anybody after the first time I found out, but this time I have spoken to a close friend and a therapist and also my mum. It has helped a lot.'

'Get support from a specialist therapist in order to fully understand the addiction and its impact on you and be able to talk to someone close, otherwise it feels a burden you have to carry alone.'

'Seek help and find others in your situation.'

'Seek individual support to deal with your emotions and focus on your own recovery.'

'Try and get counselling, see someone, do not keep it all to yourself, it doesn't mean you are a failure to seek out help, sometimes we can't do it all on our own.'

Unfortunately there are currently limited services available within the NHS (National Health Service), but hopefully this will change as sex addiction becomes more widely accepted and understood. Here are some of the most common types of therapy available within the private sector. Contact details can be found in the resources section at the end of this book:

- **Individual therapy** – this is probably the first port of call for most partners, but do make sure that you're seeing someone who has some training in sex addiction. The best starting place would be the ATSAC (Association for the Treatment of Sexual Addiction and Compulsivity) website which lists counsellors and psychotherapists who have reached approved standards of training. Some Relate centres have also completed additional training but do check with your local centre first.
- **Group courses** – some people baulk at the idea of joining a group, but it is the most effective way of breaking through the isolation and shame that so many partners experience. Being with others who know exactly how you're feeling will not only provide much-needed empathy and support in the here and now, but also for many years to come. There are a growing number of Hall Recovery Courses for Partners available around the UK and at some Relate centres.
- **12-step groups** – some partners have found peer-led 12-step groups invaluable in their recovery from sex addiction, especially those who identify as co-dependent. COSA is an organisation dedicated to the partners of sex addicts and there are a growing number around the UK as well as online, and telephone groups.
- **Online support groups** – one of my favourite online resources for partners is www.recoverynation.com. As above, COSA also provide an online support community and PoSARC (Partners of Sex Addicts Resource Center), based in the US, also provides excellent resources. Coming soon is a forum for partners on my site at www.paulahall.co.uk.

8 Identifying, avoiding and overcoming co-dependency

We looked briefly in Chapter 3 at the history of how and where co-dependency, sometimes referred to as co-addiction, came from. In this chapter we will talk more about co-dependency and, in particular, how to identify co-dependency in the context of sex and porn addiction, how to avoid it, and what to do about it if it's too late.

In the survey I undertook that accompanies this book, I was keen to find out what partners' experiences were of co-dependency. I found that 41.58 per cent of respondents had considered that they may be co-dependent or had been told they might be by a therapist or health professional. Some found the label extremely unhelpful:

'Co-dependency is the automatic assumption of most counsellors because of their treatment model. I do not identify myself as co-dependent.'

'I personally don't fit nor believe in the co-dependency or co-addiction models. I have experienced and survived prolonged trauma and abuse from my SA partner. My reactions after D-Day have been trauma symptoms stemming from survival and a need for safety. A male therapist I saw for one session, evidently used the "co-addict" model and handed me a partner worksheet saying that "wanting disclosure occurs at the height of co-dependency". The other times that it's been suggested is in a plethora of sex addiction books. It is a serious form of victim blaming, which is a factor that increases the risk of PTSD developing.'

'I don't like the term co-dependent – it is as if I enabled or let it happen in some way, which I did not, in my opinion. I was not aware of the addiction aspect until recently and several therapists had failed to diagnose this in my husband. He was extremely good at concealing the true picture.'

'I have read about and considered this but I do not think it accurately describes my situation. The "condition" which most closely approximates to how I feel is trauma and post-traumatic stress.'

'I feel very strongly that I am in no way co-dependent.'

'A therapist suggested I might be co-dependent, but in early days of the marriage the porn was milder and I thought that's what men do. The internet changed that, and my husband hid it well so I'm not sure I am co-dependent, only that I tolerated it early on.'

Of those who had been told, or thought they might be co-dependent, half of them did not believe the label was correct and, as you can see, some found it extremely unhelpful and even damaging. In part, this could be because it is so difficult to define co-dependency, and no two professionals seem to agree on what it means!

Defining co-dependency

Before you can know whether or not you're co-dependent, you need to know what it is, and that, in itself, is a challenge. Having trawled through the literature on co-dependency, I have found many differing views (Hentsh-Cowles and Brock 2013; Steffens and Rennie 2007; Tripodi 2006). What they all seem to have in common is that, broadly speaking, it is a term encompassing a whole range of behaviours that are associated with living with someone who is an active addict or an addict in recovery. In some literature the definition is so encompassing that everyone on the planet would undoubtedly find themselves somewhere on the co-dependency spectrum. If you have ever cared for someone else, or tried to help them get help, or get better, you could be co-dependent. Hence any loving partner, parent and of course people in the helping professions such as my own, could be said to be 'co-dependent'.

Co-dependency, or co-addiction is defined by some professionals as the unconscious reason why partners 'chose' to be with an addict (Hentsh-Cowles and Brock 2013). In my opinion there are two problems with this thinking. The first is that some people developed their addiction years into the relationship, often at a time that coincided with more opportunity, such as travelling with work or getting the internet. The second is that we all have unconscious, as well as conscious, reasons why we choose our partner, but that doesn't mean we choose their destructive behaviours. For example, someone who is quiet and timid might unconsciously find themselves attracted to someone who is boisterous and assertive. But if that partner goes on to become a perpetrator of domestic violence, that doesn't mean they chose to be abused. Similarly, a partner of a sex addict might have found themselves unconsciously drawn to someone who was spontaneous, charming, friendly and outgoing, but they didn't ever expect that would mean they would have multiple affairs. Or someone might unconsciously choose a partner who is similar to themselves – perhaps someone who is sexually outgoing, or sexually reserved – but again, that doesn't mean they knew they would later become addicted to internet porn or visiting sex workers.

One thing that is commonly agreed upon by professionals is that *some* partners are co-dependent and it is almost always something that they learned early in life. You are more likely to be co-dependent if you came from a family background where you were expected to look after others from an early age, or where you learned that looking after other people was important for your own safety. For example, people who were brought up in homes where there was an addiction or domestic violence or abuse may have learned that if they kept their parent happy, they were less likely to get hurt themselves. Or if they had a parent or sibling who was ill or depressed, they may have felt obliged, or have been overtly told, that others' needs were more important than their own.

As you can see, defining co-dependency is not easy as it can encompass such a wide range of conscious and unconscious thinking and behaviours and it is further confused by its similarity to a natural response to trauma.

Co-dependent or traumatised?

Over recent years it has become increasingly apparent that many of the traditional signs and symptoms of co-dependency are the same as those experienced by people who have experienced a trauma. As we explored in Chapter 4, trauma is a very natural and normal response to discovering sex addiction. Have a look at the common symptoms below:

*   **Co-dependency symptoms** – constant vigilance and preoccupation with partner's behaviours, neglecting one's own needs and self-care, feelings of anxiety, depression, low self-esteem, emptiness, helplessness and hopelessness.
*   **Trauma symptoms** – constant vigilance, intrusive thoughts and memories, difficulty sleeping and eating, losing interest in activities, feelings of anxiety, depression, low self-esteem, emptiness, helplessness and hopelessness.

As you can see, the similarities are striking, and hence an increasing number of sex addiction professionals are adopting what is known as a relational trauma model when working with partners, rather than a co-dependency model.

What is more, even if co-dependency is suspected, it is impossible to know until the trauma symptoms have subsided. Hence, no one can, or should, be considered co-dependent until a minimum of 6 months post-disclosure. This means that if you're a partner reading this book and you suspect you may be co-dependent, it may be more helpful to postpone reading the rest of this chapter until you're confident that the initial shock has well and truly worn off.

In Chapter 3, we saw how the label of co-dependent or co-addict is often unhelpful to partners as they feel they are being blamed for causing the problem. But whatever the definition, that is most certainly not the aim. There are undoubtedly some partners of sex addicts who are co-dependent, and probably have been for all of their lives. But their intentions were never to cause or maintain the pain of addiction. On the contrary, people who are co-dependent often go to extraordinary lengths to help and care for others. They are often the most loving, generous, non-judgemental, accepting and selfless people we will ever meet, and the most sacrificial and altruistic. On the surface these are, of course, admirable qualities, but the true co-dependent often sacrifices much, much more than they realise. Over time, many co-dependents, especially those living with someone with sex addiction, may lose everything, including their sense of self. When a co-dependent is losing, that is when the tables can turn and the negative character traits come to the fore. Ultimately co-dependency is about control. Caring for others gives a sense of security and stability and makes the co-dependent feel valued and loved. But if that caring is rejected or seems to be failing because the partner isn't responding, then co-dependents can become manipulative, angry and aggressive as they attempt to regain control.

Identifying co-dependency

So if all of us are somewhere on the co-dependency spectrum, and co-dependents have many very positive and enviable traits, how can you know if, or when, it is a problem? Perhaps what is more helpful than deciding whether or not someone is 'co-dependent' is to think instead about how much someone is struggling with co-dependency. In other words, rather than using the term as an identifying label for someone, we look instead at the behaviours and thinking patterns that are common in co-dependency. Crucially, we identify how they can be damaging for partners.

Co-dependent behaviours

Hypervigilance and constant checking – this is perhaps one of the most common signs that you may be co-dependent, although it is common in the early days, especially if more information is still being discovered (90 per cent). But if it is 6 months post-disclosure and you and your partner have established an accountability contract (see Chapter 11), but nonetheless, you still find yourself feeling constantly on edge, permanently preoccupied with fears and concerns about their behaviours and constantly checking up, then you are most likely struggling with co-dependency.

Although this behaviour may feel very natural, indeed it may feel like an essential survival strategy, it takes away time and emotional energy for personal recovery and leaves you continually dependent on your partner's behaviour for your sense of safety and security.

Walking on eggshells – people with co-dependency tend to be people pleasers and peace keepers, people who are terrified of rocking the boat or getting caught in conflict.

This behaviour demonstrates that there is more concern about the other's feelings and their reaction than your own needs. There are of course times when things are best left unsaid and undone, but it should be motivated by a desire to make life better for yourself and/or your relationship, rather than make life easier for someone else.

Excuses and cover-ups – if you're living with someone with addiction then it's essential that they take responsibility for the consequences of their behaviour – past, present and future. Sometimes partners can find themselves making excuses or covering up for their partner. That might mean telling white lies to save face when they've failed to live up to a responsibility, or picking up the pieces when they've let someone down. There may be occasions when this is unavoidable or it is inappropriate to disclose the truth, but it's never your responsibility to do that.

Until someone with an addiction is forced to face the consequences, it can be easier for them to continue or to stay in denial of how it impacts others. Although it may seem like the kind thing to do, it can actually help the problem to continue. What's more, it can leave you acting in ways that do not conform with your personal values and beliefs, which can further damage self-esteem and personal growth.

Overcompensation – this is similar to the above but doesn't include others. For example, it may mean compensating for financial losses by working longer hours or limiting personal spending. Or it might mean doing more work around the home or taking on additional family responsibilities to compensate for time taken by the addiction or recovery.

There is a fine balance to be found here. Assuming you want to stay in the relationship, it is important to be supportive of your partner and mindful of their attempts to get into recovery and rebuild their life. But, as above, it is equally important that they are taking full responsibility for the consequences of their addiction and recovery. Overcompensating can be exhausting and leave little time for rebuilding your own life and your recovery.

Difficulty with boundaries – a common trait of co-dependency is difficulty maintaining boundaries. This can go one of two ways. Most commonly it means having poor boundaries. Not sticking to things you've said, being unable to say no or doing things you don't want to do, such as having sex when you're really not in the mood. For some it means having boundaries that are too rigid, trying to control the other's behaviour with watertight guidelines that may be impossible to adhere to. There is more about boundaries in the next section on avoiding co-dependency.

Self-harming – regrettably this is common during the initial trauma of discovery (26.73 per cent), but if self-harming behaviours continue, or have always been around, then it may be a co-dependent behaviour. Co-dependents are often out of touch with their own needs and their own healthy ability to self-soothe. Hence they may self-injure or hurt themselves in other ways such as drinking too much, taking drugs, over or under eating, compulsive spending or sexually acting out themselves.

The negative consequences of this are hopefully obvious, but it can often be justified as a way of coping or by saying 'it's not as bad as what they're doing'. Or sometimes it's a way of getting revenge by letting them see what you've been driven to. But in reality, you're the one that is being hurt, and you can only recover by identifying your needs and finding healthy ways of meeting them.

Co-dependent thinking

If s/he knows how much I love him/her, s/he'll change – we've all been brought up with the myths about love. You know the ones: 'love is enough', 'love conquers all', 'love changes everything'. There is no doubt that love can be a great motivator for change, but it is not enough. Think about it rationally; if it were enough, then how did you end up here in the first place? Love does not cure addiction.

The problem with this thinking is that it makes it all about you and puts you in an impossible position of having to be the perfect spouse at all times. The truth is that partners of people with addiction sometimes hate their partners. I know that sounds harsh, but it's true. And that is one of the consequences that people with addiction have to live with. You have been hurt terribly and at times you will not feel love. That doesn't mean your relationship is doomed or inevitably your partner will act out. You have to be real about your emotions and be yourself. They have to choose to stop because 'they' want to, not because you love them.

I have to be perfect to be loved – this is similar to the above in as much as it puts a huge pressure on the partner to always be loving. But it goes further in as much as the thinking will most certainly have pre-dated the addiction and is likely to be apparent in every relationship.

No one is perfect, and healthy relationships develop where we are loved in spite of our shortcomings. If you can only believe you're loved when you're perfect, you are doomed to fail.

If s/he knows how much they've hurt/angered me, s/he'll change – some partners find themselves trapped by pain and anger and can begin to use this as a weapon to try and keep their partner in recovery.

These feelings are natural on occasions, but if you adopt this as a principle for the rest of your life then you're most certainly being co-dependent. You are not responsible for their recovery – not how you think, feel or behave. It is up to them. Furthermore, this thinking will slowly lead to bitterness and resentment and rob you of the happiness you deserve.

I am essential to my partner's recovery – in other words, my partner is 'dependent' on me for their recovery. This is the root of co-dependent thinking: 'if I wasn't here', 'if I didn't do what I do', 'if I don't . . .', then my partner will not recover'. Beneath this thinking often lies a desperate need to be needed.

True recovery from addiction comes when the addict wants to recover for themselves, regardless of whether or not their relationship continues. While they may benefit from your support and encouragement, neither of you should be trapped in the relationship by dependency.

My way is the right way – another common trait of co-dependency is trying to control the recovery process by deciding what should and should not be done. Beneath this thinking lies a deep insecurity that if my partner doesn't do their recovery in a way that makes sense to me, then it can't work or maybe they're not doing it at all.

As before, true recovery needs to come from the addict, and each will find their own way. Partners need the space to focus on their recovery and leave their partner to get on with their own. There are two separate paths, and each must walk their own. There is more on this in Chapter 11.

I don't need anyone else's help – people with co-dependency can be stoically independent. They have often got so used to caring for everyone else that they are unable to see that they too have needs and can also benefit from the help of others.

If you're refusing to talk to anyone else, even an impartial professional, then this may be a sign that you are co-dependent and you have become so detached from your own needs that you no longer recognise them at all.

Tracy

Tracy was a stereotypical co-dependent. She was quiet and shy, and avoided conflict at all costs. She was an only child of a violent alcoholic who her mother finally divorced when Tracy left home. From an early age, Tracy had learned to read her father's moods and take note of how many empty bottles were left lying around. She also did everything she could to protect her mother from her father's angry outbursts by distracting her father with funny stories and games, which he loved. When she found out her husband had had multiple affairs throughout their relationship, both online and offline, she was traumatised. She stopped eating, and declined any and every social event. As the months wore on, she blamed herself for her husband's addiction and saw it as proof that she hadn't been loving and attentive enough. She doubled her efforts to keep him happy and even offered to give up her job so she could spend more time looking after him and the home. As he got into recovery, she would make spreadsheets for him to help him manage his time better. She scheduled time for him to make outreach calls, to go to support meetings and to write his journal. If he complained, she would be very hurt and plead with him that she was doing her best. She never sought help for herself and told no one.

Gary

Gary met his partner on Grindr (an adult 'hook up' site) so he knew he was into sexual variety, but once they were married he had assumed it would stop. Two years later his husband went into recovery for sex addiction, confessing that he had never quit Grindr and he had continued to meet countless men. A further 2 years passed before Gary demanded therapy for them as a couple. He described his husband as immature and not committed to his recovery because he had frequent relapses. He was sure that the only reason he attended 12-step meetings was to see other men, and Gary had secretly put a tracker on his car and monitoring software on his computer which had confirmed that he often did not tell the truth. Gary had also told all of their friends and family, including his husband's ageing mother who didn't know he was gay. Gary could see no future together, and their relationship had become a constant battleground with frequent threats to leave that never materialised. In therapy Gary was able to see that his co-dependent thinking and behaviours stemmed from a desperately insecure childhood and the only reason he stayed in the relationship was because he was terrified of being alone. He agreed to undertake individual therapy to work through his feelings and consider his future options.

Avoiding co-dependency

Almost anyone can become co-dependent, if the circumstances are right, and sufficient boundaries are not put in place to avoid it. As we saw earlier, it is now considered best practice not to label anyone as 'co-dependent' until at least 6 months after final disclosure. But if you are through that period and you're aware that many of your behaviours and much of your thinking is similar to the above, then it's essential that you put some firm boundaries in place.

Setting boundaries

There needs to be a firm boundary between your partner's recovery from addiction and your own recovery from the betrayal. You cannot 'make' your partner recover and, similarly, you cannot make them fail at their recovery. You can offer support and encouragement, and you can voice your concerns if you feel they are not sticking to promises that they've made to you, but you cannot do their recovery for them. Your focus has to remain on your needs.

Setting your boundaries means establishing what's important to you. Knowing what you need. You are perfectly entitled to tell your partner what you need, to enable you to recover from the trauma and betrayal, and you can tell them what the consequences will be if those boundaries are crossed.

Accountability and boundaries are often confused. In Chapter 11 we will talk about how you can establish accountability to help both you and your partner share a common understanding of, and agreement to, addiction recovery. But here we are talking about your personal boundaries for your recovery. It can be helpful to think of boundaries as the central reservation in a motorway. It's an essential way of avoiding a crash, but those boundaries may at times be moved if necessary, if and when circumstances change. Setting boundaries is an essential way for you to protect yourself. The most effective boundaries are practical ones that are simple to maintain and obvious to everyone. Your boundaries may be around things such as:

- **Physical contact** – partners vary enormously in how much physical and sexual contact they want. If you want to sleep in separate rooms and have no physical contact, then that is a boundary that you can put in place. However, you can't insist on physical contact unless your partner also wants it.
- **Emotional contact** – some partners can find it very difficult to talk about what's happening and may find it helpful to set some boundaries as to when and where conversations take place. In addition there may be particular emotions that are hard to deal with, for example, a partner may say that they do not want to be confronted with anger from their partner or to listen to their feelings of regret and guilt, and may ask that their partner takes these feelings elsewhere for the time being.
- **Your home environment** – we talked about the home environment in Chapter 5, on identifying triggers, so if you haven't done the exercise there yet, now would be a good time to do it. It may be that you decide you don't want mobile phones or internet devices to be checked while you are in the house, or only when in your presence. Or another boundary might be agreeing on what will be watched on television and who is invited into the home.
- **Your family and friends** – some friends and family members can be an essential support, but if there are certain people that a partner finds hard to be around, then a boundary may be set that they are not seen for at least the next few months. It's important, of course, that children are protected from any decisions, so stepchildren may be seen outside of the home temporarily or grandparents may be visited at their home rather than yours.
- **Your joint finances** – most partners find it helpful to set boundaries around their finances, and may request that no withdrawals are made without their knowledge and that both bank and credit card statements are made available.

In Chapter 11 we talk about how to set up an accountability contract that can provide a joint framework for rebuilding trust and repairing the relationship, which can incorporate some of these boundaries. But remember, these boundaries are about you and your self-care and are there to protect you and your emotional recovery and ensure that you focus on your needs, not just on your partner's.

Overcoming co-dependency

If having read through this chapter you've become aware that you have many co-dependent thoughts and behaviours, then this is something that you will most likely want to address to enable you to move on with your life. In the last two chapters we talked about the 'Three Cs' – you didn't Cause it, you can't Control it, and you can't Cure it. For people with co-dependency, this needs to become a mantra. As we saw earlier, the roots of co-dependency often come from a dysfunctional childhood, and until these issues are addressed, the truth of the Three Cs just can't sink in. Trying to rebuild your life with a sexually addicted partner, without addressing co-dependency, is like trying to build a house on jelly.

The SURF acrostic is also equally important for people with co-dependency. Partners need to Survive the trauma, Understand their cycle of reaction, Repair self-identity, and Face the future, but you need to expect that it will take longer to do this work.

Someone with co-dependency might never have had the opportunity to build a positive sense of self-identity. It is common for that identity to have always been based on the approval and love of others. So rather than 'repairing' self-identity, it may be a case of starting from scratch. Because of this poorly developed sense of self, it is also likely that someone with co-dependency will find it particularly difficult to face the future – especially if that future means being alone. There are many excellent books written to help partners overcome co-dependency which you'll find in the resources section at the end of this book.

I'm going to leave the final words in this chapter to one of the partners, who offers this advice – advice that, if followed, can both avoid, and help to overcome co-dependency.

You may feel as if you want to decode and understand every last thing about your partner to explain their behaviour. You can't. You can learn a lot, which will certainly help immensely, but you won't understand it all. But if you put that energy and effort into yourself, you will come closer to finding the reward you seek and deserve. Like loss and grief, all we can seek to do with pain is learn how to accept what we cannot change and live at peace. Empower yourself, do not try to fix your partner. That will not ease your pain. Let go. The addiction is theirs to address, not yours.

Part III

The couple relationship – make or break?

'The true test of a relationship comes only after people have seen the worst of you.'

William Murphy

In this final part we will explore the impact of sex addiction on the couple relationship and will start by looking at the many things that need to be considered before making the decision to stay, leave or give the relationship more time. In Chapter 10 we look at how the impact on the relationship depends, in part, on both the partner's and the addict's response as well as the length and stage of the relationship. There is also practical advice on improving day-to-day communication and avoiding conflict. Chapter 11 focuses on the essentials required for rebuilding trust and also explains the importance and role of 'therapeutic disclosure', detailing how to create an accountability contract. Our final chapter is devoted to the subject of sex and sexuality, and starts by answering some of the common questions and fears that partners have. We then move on to consider what 'healthy' sexuality means and end with some advice for achieving it.

The couple relationship –
make or break?

9 Can the relationship survive?

For many partners, knowing the future of the relationship feels like the most urgent decision they have to make. If you've turned directly to this chapter and you're still within the first 6 months of disclosure or discovery then I would strongly advise that you turn back to Chapter 1. Ending a relationship is a big decision, especially if you have children, and you deserve to ensure you're in the strongest place emotionally and psychologically before you make that decision.

In this chapter we're going to look at reasons why you may choose to stay in your relationship, and reasons why you might leave. We will also look at things you can do to minimise the impact of separation if you have children. But first we are going to look at good reasons to postpone making a decision.

Reasons to postpone making a decision

You're angry, afraid and hurting most of the time – making a decision about the future of your relationship will inevitably be guided by your emotions, but it should not be based on it. If you're in a state of high emotion then now is not the time to make a decision that will affect both you, and those you love, for the rest of your life. Give yourself more time for these strong feelings to subside before you make the decision.

You had always been happy in your relationship before discovering the addiction – if your relationship had fundamentally been a happy one before you found out about the addiction then it may not be worth sacrificing everything that was good. If your partner is unable to get into recovery and maintain recovery, you may change your mind, but for now it may be sensible to wait and see.

You haven't had full disclosure – it's difficult to make a decision about leaving or staying unless you know what it is you're leaving behind or staying with. We talk more in the next chapter about disclosure.

Your partner is fully committed to recovery – if your partner is working hard at their recovery and all the evidence shows that they're doing well, then it may be too soon to decide to leave or stay. You will never get irrefutable proof that the addiction is in the past, but, nonetheless, you may prefer to wait and see how the next few months pan out.

There are signs of improvement – they may be small and far between, but if you feel that your relationship is improving and continuing to improve, then perhaps it will do so even more if you give it more time.

Children – deciding to stay 'for the sake of the children' is a controversial issue and as well as considering the impact of separation, you also need to consider what your children will learn about relationships if you stay. But if you feel strongly that separating now would be detrimental to your children, then that's a very good reason not to do it.

Financial considerations – some people simply can't afford to separate, while others know it would be a significant strain on both individual and personal circumstances. In the short term, the cost of separation may be too great and hence staying together may make more sense.

Before moving on to look at reasons to stay, it's important to understand what staying with a sex addict means. Back in Chapter 2 we explored the meaning of recovery and saw that it is a process, not a one-off event. It is important that partners understand that addiction is unlikely to ever be over, but rather that the process of recovery will become part of the relationship. Some partners stay in the relationship with the assumption that the addiction will be left in the past and there will be a time in the future when it might even be forgotten. This may be true for a few, but, for most, staying together will mean incorporating your partner's recovery needs into your day-to-day life. The recovery journey is different for every individual and hence first on our list is 'understanding your partner's recovery'.

Reasons to stay

Below are a list of statements that might help partners to decide that the relationship, in spite of everything, is too good to leave. They are not in any order of importance, and even if you agree with all of them, that won't mean that there isn't still a lot of relationship rebuilding to be done.

You understand what 'recovery' means – if you've read the books and/or spoken to professionals and discussed with your partner what recovery is going to involve, and you feel reasonably OK with that, then you may choose to stay.

You're willing to accept your partner's recovery needs – if your partner is in recovery and has shared with you what they need to maintain their recovery – and how it will affect you and your relationship – and you're able to accept and accommodate this, then your relationship has an excellent foundation for repair and growth.

You both still love each other – unfortunately 'love does not conquer all' but if you still love your partner, and in spite of what has happened, still have some belief that they love you, then there is still hope that the relationship can survive.

Your partner has acknowledged responsibility and wants to change – if your partner has accepted full responsibility for the addiction and committed to recovery, then you may decide that the future can be very different from your past.

You're still able to talk to each other and enjoy each other's company – if, in spite of the addiction, you're still able to communicate in a healthy and meaningful way and you still enjoy being together, then you have a good solid basis from which to grow.

You continue to share many happy memories – if you've been in your relationship for a long time and you have shared many good times and family times together, then you may decide that is too much to throw away.

You both share the same goals for the future – a shared sense of history is important for many couples, but even more important is a shared view of the future. If you still share hopes, dreams and ambitions for the future and are willing to work together to achieve them, then it is probably worth giving it a go.

You would lose something really special if you weren't together – there are many things that make a good relationship, and some couples share things with a partner that are unique and especially important to them. That may be a business, a spiritual faith, parenting, a political view or perhaps a particularly good sex life. If it's something that is very important to you, then you may not want to risk losing it.

You don't know why you want to go – if the only reason you're thinking of leaving is because you feel you should, or others have told you that you should, then you will almost certainly regret leaving.

Reasons to leave

You may notice that there are more statements below to indicate leaving than staying or waiting. That is not because there are necessarily more reasons to leave, but because the reasons may include ones that are out of your control, such as your partner. Ultimately it takes two people to make a relationship survive sex addiction, so you may choose to leave because of your partner's decisions.

Your partner continues to deny their sex addiction – rebuilding trust (which we'll explore in depth in the next chapter) is essential for a relationship to survive. If your partner doesn't even accept that they are a sex addict, then there is no way trust can be rebuilt.

Your partner refuses to accept responsibility for their addiction – similar to the above, if your partner continues to blame you or their circumstances for their behaviour rather than accepting responsibility for the choices they have made, then it's unlikely they will get into recovery and change.

Trial separation

Some partners find that a trial separation for an agreed amount of time gives them the distance they need to clarify their thinking. Moving out of a highly charged emotional situation may provide you with the space you need to focus on surviving the trauma and rebuilding your self-esteem. It may also provide the space to reflect on what you want for your future. If you choose this option, it's important that you're clear about the purpose of the separation and have communicated that with your partner. You'll also need to think about whether and how you'll communicate with your partner during the break and, of course, what you'll tell the children if you have them.

Your partner refuses to work at the cause of the addiction – recovering from addiction isn't simply about stopping behaviours, but working on the root causes of the addiction. If your partner is refusing to develop a deeper understanding of what led them into addiction and to work on resolving those issues, then you may decide that the risk of relapse is too great.

There has been violence or domestic abuse within your relationship – no matter where your partner is, in terms of recovery, if there has been any violence or emotional, sexual or psychological abuse within your relationship then you should seriously consider leaving now. Regrettably, evidence shows that domestic violence and abuse gets worse over time, not better.

The relationship was in difficulty before discovering the addiction – it may be that discovering sex addiction is the last straw for you and your relationship. Some relationships improve in terms of intimacy and communication once addiction has been revealed, but if there were already many difficulties, you may decide that it is just not worth the effort.

You can't or won't forgive your partner – forgiveness is a long and painful process, as we explored in the last chapter, and you may not be fully there yet. But unless you forgive at some time, you'll be left to live with bitterness and resentment. No relationship can survive unless the pain of the past can at some time be left behind.

Your partner can't or won't forgive themselves – it is understandably difficult for partners to acknowledge how important it is for the addict to be able to eventually forgive themselves. But not doing so will result in an unequal relationship where your partner permanently feels ashamed and inferior.

Staying will mean sacrificing something really important to you – if staying in your relationship with someone in recovery would mean giving up something really important to you, such as certain friends, hobbies or sexual behaviours, then you may decide it's not worth the sacrifice.

Staying would mean compromising your values – this is similar to the above, but goes even deeper. If the only way to make the relationship work would mean changing your value system, such as keeping information from others, or ending some relationships, then you may decide that your personal integrity is more important.

You no longer respect or like your partner – love is an emotion that ebbs and flows, but if you no longer have any positive feelings towards your partner and can't respect them as a human being, your relationship has little chance of surviving.

Your partner doesn't respect or like you – if your partner treats you in a way that indicates that they don't respect your needs or value you for what you bring to the relationship, then it may be time to walk away.

You're scared of what other people will say if you end it – many partners worry about the social stigma of ending a relationship, especially if they don't want to share the true reasons why. This is understandable, but inevitably it will leave you feeling trapped and drain away energy for making the relationship work.

You're just waiting for someone else – you may be holding a fantasy that somewhere out there is someone better. Indeed there may be, but there is no guarantee that a new partner wouldn't bring a whole host of new problems. If you know you want to leave, then leaving now would be the fairest thing on both you and your partner.

You're afraid of being alone – many people stay in relationships because they are scared of being alone, but regrettably that leaves people staying out of 'need' rather than 'want' and can lead to further resentment. There is only one way to beat the fear of being alone, and that is to leave, and prove that you can do it.

You just don't care anymore – indifference is the biggest killer of relationships, not blazing arguments or constant bickering, but reaching a point where you can't even be bothered to argue anymore. If this describes your relationship then it's probably time to muster up the energy to leave.

Considering children's needs

If you have children, then discovering that your partner is a sex addict, whether or not s/he is also their parent – who may also be their father – will impact them. Children of every age pick up on the emotions in the house, even if they know nothing of what's going on. This means that your children will almost certainly have been affected by the discovery of sex addiction, whatever decision you make about the future of your relationship. In Chapter 4 we looked at the difficult topic of telling children, and we look at this in more depth in Chapter 11, but whatever you have said, by way of explanation of your current situation, may also affect how your children react to the decision to separate, or stay together.

If you've got children, deciding to separate will affect their lives forever. The harsh reality is that you'll be making a decision that they will have to live with for the rest of their life, whether they like it or not. Getting through a separation and adapting to the inevitable life changes it brings is tough for anyone, but for children it's even harder.

But kids do survive separation. Research shows that children are most adversely affected by conflict and lack of contact with both parents. This means that, as parents, you will have to do everything you can to ensure you keep disagreements to a minimum and to ensure that there is regular contact with both of you. It is understandable that emotions will be running high, but those emotions need to be kept separate from the decisions that you make about your children's welfare. Whatever your partner may have done, you are responsible for ensuring that every action you take is in the best interests of your children. Remember, the relationship you have with your partner may be over, but your relationship with your children is for life.

We know that a secure family unit forms the foundation of a child's healthy psychological and emotional development, and when you remove that structure the impact can be devastating. But staying together doesn't necessarily mean that children will have the safe and happy home-life they deserve. Whatever decision you make as a partner will affect your children, and this is another very good reason not to make any knee-jerk decisions based on high emotion. Take time to let strong emotions subside, and explore your options. Also talk to friends and family who know you as a family and who you can trust to care about everyone's needs.

Below are a few things that partners said regarding their relationships when asked what advice they would give to others. Some may give you hope, others will not:

'Be strong and know yourself and what you want from the relationship once the truth of his behaviour and actions is out. Give yourself time and space away from him to decide if you want to work to save the relationship or you're better off without him.'

'Take the time to listen, learn and talk about it. It is gut-wrenching but if you value your relationship, you'll have to do it.'

'Leave your partner – they won't change.'

'Take your time, don't make hasty decisions.'

'Get counselling and don't make any hasty decisions. People can be judgemental so try not to tell anyone until you have decided what is right for you.'

'If something's worth having it's worth fighting for. Don't expect an easy ride, it's a long difficult one. You need to learn to fall in love again with someone who has hurt and betrayed you in the worst possible way.'

'Do not give up hope. You and your partner must educate yourselves about sex addiction. Seek professional help individually and also as a couple. Be patient.'

'Leave him as soon as you find out what he's capable of.'

'In order to be able to continue your life well, to give your partner the freedom to look to the future and recover from their addiction, you must be able to separate the addiction and addictive behaviour from the person. Until you can do this, you will continually be looking backwards at pain, hurting yourself and hating your partner for what is in the past. It's not possible to forget it but you can look forwards to the future, in the way that your partner is trying to. This, I believe, will give you the best chance of coping.'

'Think hard about the good qualities that you formerly saw in this man. If it is worth persevering with him, you may have to be very patient; it took my husband a long time to seek change wholeheartedly.'

Ultimately, no one but you can decide whether or not your relationship can survive, and there are no guarantees. But if you want it to survive, the only thing you can do is commit to working at it and see what happens. The following chapters are devoted to exploring what might be required to make the relationship work.

10 How sex addiction impacts couple relationships

In Part II we focused on how sex addiction impacts partners, but it also has a profound impact on the couple relationship too. Many couples find themselves struggling even to co-exist in the same house and look after the home and children. Others find themselves endlessly, and exhaustingly, talking about the problem, and a few attempt to continue as if nothing has happened. This chapter will explore the factors that influence how a relationship is impacted, as well as provide suggestions for how to manage in the early weeks and months.

What influences the impact?

The way a partner responds is, of course, one of the biggest influences on how much a relationship is affected, but so too is how the person with the addiction responds to the disclosure or discovery, and how they react to the partner's reaction.

The impact on the couple relationship is also influenced by the length and quality of the relationship, whether or not there are children, and their ages, and any other complicating factors such as other addictions, illness or recent bereavements. It is perhaps stating the obvious, but a couple relationship that is already on the rocks, or experiencing difficulties in other areas, is less likely to survive sex addiction, whereas a couple that have a strong and loving relationship, who have good communication skills and a shared commitment to the future, are better positioned to survive the trauma.

Having said that, every couple relationship is, of course, completely different, and hence the impact on the couple will also be different. What follows in this chapter is an exploration of the main factors that impact a couple relationship.

The partner's reaction

In Chapter 4 we focused exclusively on the partner's reaction and highlighted that, in the early days, most partners experience a roller coaster of painful emotions. What those emotions are, how long they last, and, most importantly, how they are expressed will have a significant impact on the relationship. For many partners, the first reaction is almost always a traumatised one that is driven by the need for personal survival, and how their feelings and behaviours affect the couple relationship are secondary. But as time moves on, a partner's reaction can play a significant role in how well the couple are able to relate and work through the necessary issues to get into recovery as individuals, and whether or not the relationship will survive.

Most partners experience extreme anger and feelings of personal betrayal and disgust when sex addiction is disclosed, and it is important that there is space to share and express those feelings in a healthy way. But for the couple relationship to function, even if just in the short term, there also need to be times when partners are able to detach from those feelings and communicate at a more cognitive level. There is more about this in Chapters 4 and 5. This is especially important when there are children involved and decisions need to be made about how to operate as a family.

The addict's reaction

The person with the addiction is nearly always streets ahead of their partner when it comes to their emotional reaction. Although addicts can also experience extremely powerful emotions, especially shame, guilt and fear of losing the relationship, what they normally don't have is the same degree of shock. For those addicts who have conducted their addiction within the bubble of a secret 'other' world, the collision of their addict life and real life can be experienced as a significant shock, but it rarely lasts as long as the shock experienced by partners.

This absence of shock often leaves the person with the addiction ready to move on long before a partner is ready. Once the story has been told, whether that's an edited version or the full story (more in the next chapter), many addicts feel a sense of relief and an urgency to move positively into the future and leave the addicted life behind. But this is not possible until both the addict and the partner are in a similar place and both feel ready. In addition to the discrepancies in shock, there are some addict reactions to discovery or disclosure that can be particularly damaging for the couple relationship, namely:

- **Denial** – there are many different levels of denial, and it is likely that an addict will experience at least some denial in the early stages of recovery. But denial that continues can make it impossible for the couple to communicate at any meaningful level. Denial may be about the behaviours, about being an addict, or about the severity of the addiction or the amount of pain caused. While an addict continues in denial it is almost impossible to demonstrate the attitudes and changes that are necessary to rebuild trust.

- **Defensiveness** – some addicts become very defensive about their behaviours and can become aggressive and blaming. While this behaviour is not at all helpful, it can be useful to understand that this is usually a defence against extreme feelings of shame and guilt, and is usually a temporary response. Nonetheless, while defensiveness continues it can be particularly difficult to communicate as a couple.

- **Miraculously cured** – there are a few people with addiction who say that being discovered has given them the wake-up call they needed to stop their behaviour and stay 'stopped'. For some partners this may initially sound like great news and they may share the initial relief that the problem appears to be over and in the past. But over a period of time doubts tend to creep in and many partners find themselves questioning why the addict didn't give up years ago if it was really that easy? And there are still many unanswered questions that the addict may not be able to address unless they have been into some kind of treatment or therapy. On the surface the 'miraculous cure' often looks just too good to be true, for partners, and often for good reason.

- **Wounded wretch** – some addicts find themselves trapped in shame and despair at what they've done and adopt a position within the relationship of the 'hang dog'. They may feel that the consequence of their behaviour is that they have no rights to anything anymore and they must be compliant with any request or demand, no matter how unreasonable. Some partners welcome this at first, but it soon becomes tiring and frustrating. Many fear the honesty of anything they're told or witness as being something that's done 'just to please or placate me' and it can be particularly difficult to justifiably share feelings of anger and grief with someone who appears so mortally wounded.

The ideal response from the addict is to be open, honest, remorseful, empathic and committed to recovery. There is more on this in Chapter 11, on rebuilding trust, but, in short, this attitude enables partners to express their feelings and allows the couple to communicate honestly about their hopes and fears for the future.

Length and life stage of the relationship

Some relationships are more sensitive to the blow of sex addiction than others. If you've recently moved home, experienced a significant illness or if either of you has changed jobs or lost their job, then you may already be feeling the discomfort of change, and if you've recently had a baby or been bereaved then you may be feeling especially vulnerable. There are some times in life when we lean on our partners more than others, and if you are in one of those stages in your relationship, then sex addiction can feel like a bigger blow, and both of you may feel especially fearful of losing the familiar comfort of each other.

The length of a relationship also has an impact on how a couple respond, but both long and short relationships bring different benefits and challenges. If it's a new relationship then there may be less shared history to hold on to but, conversely, there may be stronger hopes and dreams for the future together. A couple who have been together for many years are more likely to have weathered other storms together and thereby built more resilience and better conflict management techniques. Alternatively, there may be a history of dysfunction and discord, and sex addiction may be the proverbial last straw. Couples with children may be more inclined to want to avoid the damaging effect that separation could have on their family, but if parenting has been a source of conflict, the addiction may give the incentive to separate.

Every relationship is unique but, generally speaking, couples with children will take more time deciding whether or not the relationship can be restored. However, for all, it is the quality of the relationship before discovery that is the biggest factor.

Quality of the relationship

Some people know they have a good relationship and that fact does not change when addiction is discovered or disclosed. There is a firm foundation of shared values and commitment to the future and the addiction is an unwanted intruder that the couple chooses to fight side by side. For some couples, the relationship has never been good or it has been deteriorating over the years, and discovering sex addiction finally ends it. It is perhaps stating the obvious to say that a relationship that is already in difficulty is going to experience the most negative impact of sex addiction.

One of the most common and confusing scenarios is the relationship that had always 'appeared' to be really good. Many partners talk of having a relationship that their friends had envied, or being the couple that other couples go to for advice when their own marriages are floundering. But when addictive behaviours are discovered, the previous years can feel like a farce. And for the person with the addiction, while they have always known their secret, they are often terrified that the happy relationship they've always enjoyed will now be meaningless and lost. It can be especially difficult for these couples to disentangle the good bits of the relationship from the addiction and ensure that their relationship strengths are not poisoned and killed. The key to achieving this is to ensure that both the person with the addiction and the partner get help and support for themselves, as well as couple counselling to help them move on.

Unconscious couple collusions

All couples get together because of the things they love about each other, and for deeper unconscious reasons that often do not come to the surface until the relationship gets into difficulty. These are known as unconscious collusions and they come with benefits for both partners. Some unconscious collusions might be the socialite and the introvert, one learns how to become more outgoing while the other becomes better at enjoying their own company. Some unconscious collusions are unique to the couple, but there are some common styles that present in sex addiction.

These collusions are more common in couples where an attachment-induced addiction is present, as early attachment difficulties will almost certainly have affected mate choice, either preferring to be in a relationship with someone who is completely different and represents the opposite, or with someone who is familiar. For example, someone who was brought up with unreliable parenting might end up in a relationship with a partner who is also unreliable. Or conversely, they may choose a partner who is so devoted and attentive that at times the relationship may feel suffocating. Someone from a background that was strict and punitive may find themselves with a partner who has strong opinions and boundaries, or maybe a partner who struggles to hold a view or make a decision. Whatever the collusion, addiction will bring it to the fore and challenge it. Other common collusions can include the following:

- **parent/child** – where one person takes responsibility for fun and spontaneity and the other is responsible for the practical issues. Sometimes it is the addict who is the child-like one, and discovery results in a partner taking an even stronger parenting role, either trying to fix the broken child or chastising it. Conversely sometimes the partner has always taken the child-like role and the addiction has been the place where the addict has let go of their parental responsibility and 'played'.

- **Idol/worshipper** – where one partner is put on a pedestal as the strong, successful and competent one and the other stays in the background giving support and encouragement. When the addict is in the role of idol, the discovery of addiction can be a massive shock to the partner who had believed their partner could do no wrong. When the partner has been the idol, the addiction is sometimes the place the worshipper goes to for their own adoration.

- **Victim/rescuer** – where one person frequently plays the role of someone who is either currently being persecuted by someone or something, or has been in the past, and the other looks after them and helps them to feel better and stronger. This collusion is most common in couples who have come from backgrounds with abuse, bullying or domestic violence. Both will have unconsciously vowed never to become an abuser themselves but inadvertently find themselves permanently trapped either as a victim of life's circumstances or a rescuer and caretaker of another's needs. Addiction often throws the balance of power, and couples can find themselves endlessly oscillating between feeling victimised and wanting to rescue or attack each other.

- **Brother/sister** – these couples are often the best of friends but they have never had a good sexual relationship. At an unconscious level, these kinds of relationships can seem like a safe place for the addiction to hide, and it can look like a very successful and intimate relationship. The discovery of sex addiction can be a huge shock to partners and may push them further into being sexual avoidant. But, for a few, the discovery is met with some relief as they no longer have to suppress their sexual needs.

- **Addict/co-dependent** – this is, of course, one of the most common collusions in addiction, but more so in other addictions than in sex and porn addiction. A co-dependent is someone who stays with an addict in spite of the negative consequences it is having on their life and focuses all their attention on helping and fixing their partner. If you have been living as a partner of a sex addict for a long time then this may describe you, or if you've known your partner has had other addictions in the past and you have always supported them.

It is important to remember that these collusions are mutually agreed, even if they're unspoken and unconscious. Hence it is not possible for one partner to take on a position of child unless there is a parent within the relationship to pick up the pieces, and you can't be co-dependent unless there is someone who lets you play that role. It is never one partner's fault, but rather a system that evolved, often from early family dysfunctions. There is more on co-dependency in Chapter 8.

The impact on communication and day-to-day living

One of the challenges for couples affected by sex addiction is that their needs of each other are very different. Both need reassurance, comfort and support, but they are in very different places. These differences stem in part from being at very different places on the journey. Often the person with the addiction is relieved that the truth is finally out and they are ready to move on into recovery and recommitting to the relationship. But the partner is still reeling from the shock, and may not be able to even think about moving forward, let alone doing it.

- **Partners' needs** – space to air their feelings, including rage and despair, empathy and understanding of how they feel. They need to know why the addiction happened, to know why they were deceived, to know that the full story has been revealed. They need reassurance that it is not their fault, demonstrations of remorse and guilt, proof that the addiction is over, reassurance that the addict will never act out again, and support to get through day by day. They need to be loved.

- **Addicts' needs** – space to share their feelings, including their struggle with recovery, encouragement and support to get into recovery, reassurance that the relationship will survive, assurance that they're still a good person, support to get through day-by-day, and to be loved.

For couples who have always been close and supportive, these times can be especially challenging, and both can feel betrayed by the other that they're unable to meet their needs. For those who have had difficulty communicating in the past, these disparate needs can become a significant and regular source of conflict.

Improving communication

In the early days after disclosure, many couples benefit from agreeing what couple therapists call 'ventilation sessions'. The objective of ventilation sessions is to create a contained space for communication. This means that both of you have agreed how often you will talk, when and where. It is a time when you can be alone and uninterrupted, awake and sober!! This latter point is crucial. Many couples find themselves talking, or arguing, late into the night after numerous alcoholic drinks. As the hours roll by, and the drink rolls in, the conversations become more and more destructive. Another common problem is that there seems to be no time for just getting on with life, and every available moment is spent talking endlessly about the addiction. It can feel as if the addiction is contaminating everything. Ventilation sessions stop this from happening.

How to set a ventilation session

Most couples find it beneficial to agree two or three ventilation sessions a week, lasting a maximum of 2 hours at a time. Some prefer daily sessions of 45 minutes. The agreement is that you will both have an opportunity to talk and listen during this time, asking questions, sharing feelings, and giving feedback. In the early days the sessions may not feel very constructive at all, but they should at least provide some sense of containment and control. By incorporating other good communication techniques they should in time become more productive as emotions begin to subside. In addition to the ventilation sessions, most couples find it beneficial to see a couple counsellor as well, who can act as an arbitrator as well as offer advice on improving communication and minimising conflict.

For more information and help on improving your relationship do get a copy of the very excellent (written by guess who), *Improving your relationship – for dummies.*

In addition to setting ventilation sessions, couples can help to avoid situations spiralling into conflict by establishing strategies for when partners are triggered or when situations arise where painful feelings are evoked. Couples often find that times of relative peace and tranquillity are shattered by external circumstances, such as when the person with the addiction has failed to stick to a commitment, or when a wound has been poked by someone or something. For example, it can happen when an article on the news is about prostitution, a dinner party conversation includes porn or infidelity, or someone attractive is seen when out together. There is a three-point plan for both partners that can help to calm the situation quickly.

The partner needs to:

1   **Name what has happened** – explain what has occurred and take responsibility for the feelings that have been evoked, without feeling any need to blame, justify or apologise. For example, 'I am feeling angry because you are late' or 'I am upset that topics relating to your acting out have been raised', or 'I am anxious that you are looking at that person'.

2   **Put it into context** – explain that it is not just what happened now, but what it has brought up from the past. For example, 'You may have a good reason for being late, but it has reminded me of times in the past

when it was linked to your addiction', or 'I know these topics will sometimes arise but I'm struggling to manage it today', or 'I realise you may not be looking at that person, but it reminds me that in the past you did'.

3 **Request clarification and/or reassurance** – that may mean asking for an explanation of what has happened, or simply asking for reassurance. For example, 'please explain to me why you were late and why you didn't let me know', or 'I would like us to find ways of avoiding these topics in the future or changing the topic immediately. If we can't, then I would like you to put your arm round me to acknowledge you know this is hard for me', or 'were you looking at that person, and if yes, why?'

The person with the addiction needs to:

1 **Fall on their sword** – in other words, say sorry, sorry, sorry, and demonstrate remorse for what's happened, even if it's not their fault, without justification or excuse. For example, 'I'm sorry I was late and didn't let you know, that was wrong of me', or 'I'm sorry that you had to hear that topic raised', or 'I am sorry that we are in a place where someone triggering was around'.

2 **Validate current and past feelings** – demonstrate awareness that difficult feelings have been raised and that they are linked to old wounds. For example, 'you have every right to be upset with me for being late because of what it must bring up for you', or 'topics like that must be very painful for you because they remind you of what I have done', or 'I understand that attractive people can be triggering to you because I have betrayed you in the past'.

3 **Reassure** – when a partner is triggered they are often thrown into old feelings of powerlessness and hurt and need to be reassured, even if angry and shouting, 'I will work harder at not being late in the future and will keep you informed', or 'I want you to know that when difficult topics come up I am aware of how painful it is for you and I will do my best to avoid it or comfort you', or 'if there are attractive people around I will try to remember not to look in their direction so you can feel confident that my focus and attention is on you and you alone'.

It often takes quite a lot of practice for these steps to work and it is important to understand that they are not dependent on each other. Even if a partner forgets their three steps and becomes angry and accusing, the situation can be calmed down by the person with the addiction.

The impact on children

Children of any age are affected by sex addiction. Even those who you are confident will have no idea what's going on, will have picked up a change in atmosphere in the house. Older children will definitely know that something is going on, even if they can't name it. Research has shown that nearly a third of adolescent children were already aware of their parents' acting out before disclosure (Black *et al.* 2003) and hence it is clear that something almost certainly needs to be said to answer the question, whether articulated or not, 'what's going on?'.

All parents are faced with the difficult dilemma of what to tell children and when to tell them. As we saw in Chapter 4, when children learn through anger or another kind of inappropriate or unplanned disclosure, then it can be damaging. But saying nothing can also be damaging and can continue a culture of secrecy and isolation within the family. Deciding what to tell children will of course depend on their age. Small children may simply need reassurance that although mummy and daddy are not getting on well at the moment, as happens at times in all relationships, they are still there for them as parents. School-age children may need more of an explanation, especially if they have witnessed painful emotions between the two of you. Again, reassurance that the parents are coping and that they are safe is the most important thing. Older children may demand more details, especially if they are aware of infidelity or have found things on a computer, but it is important to protect them from the details of acting out behaviours and overt rage.

Many parents decide that it is best not to say much until the person with the addiction is in recovery and both are getting support. Some parents with adolescent children choose to disclose addiction and talk about the risks of hereditary factors to protect their children from making the same mistakes. Ultimately you know your children better than anyone else and it's up to you what you say and when you say it, in a way that is appropriate to them and your family unit. If in doubt, then discuss the disclosure process with a trained addiction therapist or family therapist first.

The impact on the sexual relationship

It will come as no surprise that a couple's sexual relationship is significantly affected by sex addiction, but it may surprise some to know in what ways. There is an assumption made about sex addicts, and hence also about their partners, that they come from low-sex or poor-sex relationships. As you'll see in the next chapter, sex addiction has very little to do with sex, but everything to do with addiction. This means that some couples will have enjoyed an active and varied sex life throughout the addiction, and the discovery of the acting out behaviours may devastate that. For some couples, the sexual side of their relationship has been very difficult for years but with no real explanation, and partners may have been forced to sublimate their sex drive for what they assumed was their low-sex-drive partner. For these partners, the discovery of the addiction can be a relief, and getting into recovery revitalises their sex life.

Most commonly, in the early days after discovery, couples find that their sex life swings between high desperate activity, and no interest at all, or aversion. Many couples are surprised to find that, within the trauma of sex addiction discovery, their sex life can at times become as passionate as it has ever been, or even more so. It is very common after infidelity for the betrayed person to feel highly sexual. There are a number of reasons why this can happen. In part it may be an unconscious drive to re-bond with a partner and it may also be a way to connect intimately and seek comfort. But interwoven into these periods of sexual intensity come the times of fear, loss and anger that can make sex the furthest thing from a partner's mind, and often from the addict's mind too. For some, feelings of disgust and shame can make even the thought of sexual intimacy repulsive. This yo-yoing between periods of sexual famine and feast are common in the months that follow disclosure or discovery of sex addiction and it is important that partners do not judge themselves for their conflicting feelings and desires around sex. In Chapter 12 we talk a lot more about how partners can become more in control of their sexual needs during recovery, and reclaim their sexual relationship from addiction.

Finally, there are a few partners who struggle with feelings of envy over what their partner has done. While they have been the faithful spouse, or perhaps ended extra-marital relationships and avoided other external sexual stimuli out of loyalty, their partner has been sexually experimenting in ways they had only ever dreamed of. This can be difficult for partners to talk about, since it can trigger feelings of shame for them and conflicting emotions of lust and disgust. Sexual curiosity is a very natural human phenomenon, and discovering that your partner has given into this while you've stayed true is frustrating, infuriating and confusing. Talking to a trusted friend or a therapist about these feelings is often the best way to work through them, as well as reading Chapter 12.

11 Rebuilding trust

The foundation of any successful relationship is trust, and the sexual betrayal that accompanies sex addiction profoundly damages trust. In fact, it usually obliterates it. In this chapter, we will explore the slow process of how trust can be rebuilt, and ideally both you and your partner will read it. But first let's look at why people with addiction lie so much.

Why lie?

There are lots of reasons why people lie, and while it's convenient to say that only 'bad' people lie, that's simply not the truth. We all tell lies at times. Sometimes it's to protect ourselves, sometimes it's to protect others, and when we feel our lies are justified we tend to refer to them as 'white lies'. But lies damage intimacy because they build walls of secrecy between people and stop the true self being known. Nonetheless, the truth can also hurt, and so on some occasions we withhold the full story, or our real thoughts and feelings, out of sensitivity. There are also different kinds of lies: lies of omission, in other words, not telling because no one asked; and lies of commission, when we deliberately say something that isn't true.

People with addiction generally lie out of fear, and often it has become a habit that is hard to break. They may have learned to lie in early childhood to protect themselves from consequences, or to protect a parent or the family unit. Fear is often at the root of dishonesty. For the addict, it could be fear of having to stop the behaviour, if it was known, fear of losing a loved one, or children, or friends, or financial stability, or their reputation, or indeed all of these things. People with addictions also lie to protect themselves from the pain of not living up to someone else's expectations, or their own. They are often also desperately afraid of causing even more pain to an already traumatised partner. Hence, telling the truth, as we will see in the later section on therapeutic disclosure, is often terrifying.

But there is another reason why people lie, and that is to protect their sense of autonomy. This is especially true for people who came from a family background where they were robbed of any privacy or not allowed to grow up and become a separate individual. All children tell lies and have secrets and this trait often becomes stronger in adolescence. As a child begins to form their own identity they need to keep things to themselves, and if they are not given space to do that, then rather than developing a separate private life, they will develop a secret one. Some adults continue to use lying as a strategy for having autonomy in relationships, and those needs for autonomy and separateness are greater for some than others.

All couples will have different boundaries around what they perceive as secret and private. Some will have a 24/7 open-door policy, including the toilet door; they open each other's post, share frankly about their sexual histories and fantasies, and discuss the intricacies of every conversation they have with other people. Others consider these things private and would feel embarrassed and offended if someone expected to talk to them while they were on the loo, and would feel affronted if they were not expected to maintain a friend's confidentiality. There is no right and wrong, just different. But when there has been a betrayal, the lines are much more blurred. Developing a broader understanding of the many reasons why people lie, and the deeper conscious, and unconscious, motivations, can help to rebuild trust and provide an avenue for offering reassurance that honesty really is the best policy.

Over the rest of this chapter we will look at the essential ingredients of trust and then go on to look at the importance of full, honest disclosure and explain how a 'therapeutic disclosure' can benefit both partners in the relationship. We will end this chapter with the difficult topic of how to manage relapses.

The essential ingredients of trust

No relationship can survive without trust. To feel secure, we need to know that our partner is committed to us and to the relationship, that they are the person you believe them to be and that they are there for you and will remain there through good times and bad. Trust is something that builds over time, and for people who come from a background where trust has been violated, it can take years to develop.

Unfortunately there are no fast-track ways to rebuild trust. No one moves from 'I don't trust you' to 'I do trust you' without passing through painful phases of partial trust and then crushing doubt. In the short term, all you can do is learn to live more comfortably with uncertainty.

Honesty

For trust to be rebuilt, the person with the addiction needs to commit to honesty – honesty about what's happened in the past, what's happening in the current moment, and honesty in the future. Partners also need to be honest about their feelings and their failings, helping the addict to understand their cycle of reaction and hence help them to encourage and support them when they're feeling triggered. Both partners need to become honest about their needs, both their needs in recovery and their needs from each other. Honesty needs to go far beyond the acting out behaviours. It should be assumed that acting out behaviours have stopped, or will stop, and that needs to be a prerequisite to rebuilding trust. But beyond that there needs to be a general spirit of openness and transparency about everything. That means being honest if something has been forgotten or a mistake has been made, being real about feelings, and talking about difficulties and problems rather than pretending they don't exist. This may, on the surface, sound very appealing to partners, but complete honesty and openness will mean being ready to hear things that might be challenging or painful too.

There is one area where honesty and openness can come into conflict with recovery, and that is where partners want to know all the intricate details of what happens within a therapeutic or recovery setting, for example, knowing exactly what was talked about in individual therapy, or what was said and discussed within a therapy or 12-step group. It is completely understandable that partners want to know, but within a group environment especially, this is not possible. Groups can only work within strict guidelines of confidentiality, which means that no one can talk about anyone else within the group or their story. This is essential for maintaining the anonymity of other group members and ensuring group integrity. Within individual therapy sessions it can also make it very difficult for the person with the addiction to fully open up about their concerns and feelings on the recovery journey, not necessarily because they want to hide information from their partner, but because they want to protect them. For example, an addict may have found themselves in a very difficult and triggering situation which they successfully handled and they want to share this with the therapist or group to gain encouragement and further support and guidance. They may rightly know that if they share this with their partner it may unnecessarily trigger fears and anxieties within them, even though they didn't act out. There may also be times when they want affirmation and congratulations for maintaining sobriety over a difficult period – something they rightly deserve, as giving up an addiction can be very hard work. But, understandably, most partners find it difficult to give praise for what they consider should come naturally in the first place.

Empathy

Most people are instinctively good at picking up on other people's emotions, but, unfortunately, people often aren't very good at showing it. Empathy is all about letting your partner know that you understand, not just what they said, but how they feel. It's hard to rebuild trust if you don't believe that your partner knows what you're feeling. After all, how can you trust that someone won't do something to hurt you, if they don't know when you're hurt and what hurt means to you. Fortunately, showing empathy is a skill that can be learned by developing good listening skills that make it clear that you understand not just the facts of what someone has said, but the emotional message too.

Empathy can also be communicated when the person with the addiction shows remorse and also gratitude, by expressing how aware they are of the pain that's been caused and how sorry they are for what's been done, and also by sharing how grateful they are that you are working together at rebuilding trust, and acknowledging how difficult it is.

Accountability

Some people become very concerned at the concept of 'accountability' because it can so easily be confused with 'monitoring' or 'policing'. Few partners want to feel as if it is their responsibility to monitor their partner's behaviours, but they do want some assurances that nothing untoward is going on. And they want an end to feeling insecure and frightened whenever their partner is not in their sight. The key to healthy accountability is to ensure that it is mutually agreed and is in both partners' interests. Any addict who refuses accountability measures is either not in recovery or has no remorse.

Accountability provides protection for both partners. For the person with the addiction, it protects them not only from opportunities to act out, but also from being wrongly accused. It also protects them from witnessing the pain of insecurity that can dominate partners' lives. For partners, accountability can provide evidence that the addict is committed to recovery, as well as security that they are where they say they are and doing what they say they are doing. It can also protect from some triggers, though unfortunately not all. Ideally a couple should create an accountability contract, something that is mutually agreed and written down. It is something that is much easier to achieve once you have both recognised your triggers, and after a disclosure session, which we discuss in the next section. You can either create the contract alone, or ask a therapist to help you.

The accountability contract

First list the people, places and situations that are likely to be triggering for you – see Chapter 5 if you haven't already done so. Ask your partner to write the places and situations that are most triggering for them. Now think about what each of you can do to protect your relationship from these triggers. The accountability contract can also be a tool for listing what you need to see to know that your partner is in recovery, such as attending 12-step meetings, going to therapy and keeping physically, emotionally and spiritually healthy. A typical contract might look like this:

Addict's commitments

- I will not delete history on any internet device or keep them password-protected.
- I will not use any internet device within the home unless in full view of you.
- I will leave my mobile accessible at all times and on ring.
- I will continue to attend therapy and regular support groups.
- I will use a mutually accessible online diary for all work and social appointments.
- I will make no purchase over £30 without mutual consent.
- I will not make any kind of contact with any previous acting out partners.
- I will tell you immediately if any previous acting out partners contact me.
- I will notify you immediately if I am going to be any more than 10 minutes late.
- I will not travel away overnight on business for at least the next 6 months.

Partner's commitments

- I will continue to get support from therapy and friends.
- I will request to look at your phone or any other internet device when I feel insecure.
- I will phone you on your office landline if I am feeling insecure during work hours.
- I will face-time you if I am feeling insecure and you are not near a landline.
- I will manage all our joint finances for the foreseeable future, including credit cards.

- I will say if I am feeling uncomfortable when we are socialising so we can decide what to do.

Joint commitments

- We will change the subject as soon as possible if we are out and the topic moves towards triggering material.
- We will check the content of any television programmes or films before watching.
- We will only go out to places that we are familiar with and know will be quiet.
- We will avoid beach holidays for the foreseeable future.
- We will have a weekly meeting to discuss the contract.
- We will shop online for Christmas presents this year.
- We will not celebrate Valentine's Day this year.
- We will continue in couple counselling to improve our communication.

The best accountability contracts are those that are personal to the couple. Everyone's situation is different and the more you can focus on solutions rather than problems, the better. The goal is to create something that will reduce tensions and avoid triggers for both of you so you can both focus on your recovery and moving forward.

Risk

This may seem like a strange thing to put as an essential ingredient to trust-building, but without risk there is no trust, in the same way as there is no night without day and no light without dark. If we don't take risks, then trust will never be built, as there would be no way of putting trust to the test and proving its existence.

Rebuilding trust and becoming more confident in your relationship again is not possible without taking risks. In the early days, when trust is still very fragile, those risks will be small ones. Pushing yourself too soon could put you back, but staying within your comfort zone forever will stop you from moving forward.

A good test of when it may be the right time to extend risk is when the accountability contract is beginning to feel intrusive or upsetting. For example, if your partner calling you every lunchtime is serving as more of a reminder than a reassurance, then it might be time to move to a text message instead. Or if the agreement that your partner never goes away on business without you is becoming a burden, then perhaps you can agree that single night stays will be ok. Extending rigid accountability contracts for too long can block recovery because it can become a reminder of the trust that has been broken. Letting go of the reins may feel uncomfortable at first, but gradually your trust will strengthen and you can begin to leave the acting out behaviours in the past.

The therapeutic disclosure

The term 'therapeutic disclosure' is used to describe a process whereby the full story is told by the person with the addiction to the partner. The session is done with a trained therapist whose job it is to ensure that the emotional and psychological needs of both are being cared for and that there is safety for each, once the process is complete. As we discussed in Chapter 3, many partners will have been on the receiving end of the painful process of partial and staggered disclosure, or discovery over many weeks, months or even years. During this time many couples are flooded with emotion, and sometimes what has been shared or found out can be forgotten, leaving partners unsure about what they know and what they don't know. There may also be other information that has never been revealed, either because the question hasn't been asked, or because, when it was, the truth wasn't told. A therapeutic disclosure provides the space to tell the story in full, and finally draw a line in the sand under the disclosure process.

As we've already seen, the essential ingredients for rebuilding trust are honesty, empathy and accountability, and until there has been a full disclosure, it is impossible for these to be activated. Making a full disclosure is the first, and perhaps greatest risk, but until this risk has been taken, it's much harder to take more. Both partners and addicts can be very fearful of full disclosure, but research has shown that in spite of the pain and fears, both are glad that they did it (Schneider *et al.* 1998). Furthermore, in spite of over half of partners threatening to leave, less than a quarter actually did (Corley *et al.* 2012).

The process of disclosure is one of the most widely written about in professional literature about sex addiction recovery (Black *et al.* 2003; Corley and Schneider 2003; Corley *et al.* 2012; Schneider and Levinson 2006; Schneider *et al.* 1998; Schneider *et al.* 1999), but the one most often neglected by untrained professionals. If you are in couple counselling and your therapist has not talked to you about the benefits of having a therapeutic disclosure, ask why, or find another therapist. Not only does therapeutic disclosure benefit both partners, it is very difficult, if not impossible, for couples to move forward without it.

Benefits for the partner

The benefits for partners are perhaps the most obvious, but nonetheless it may be a painful process. Some partners are already sure they know everything, but others continue to have nagging doubts. The key benefit for partners is that it allows them to make a decision about the future of the relationship based on reality and truth. It empowers them to make choices about how they respond and what they need in terms of accountability and boundaries. It also allows partners to fully commit to their own recovery rather than being preoccupied with suspicion and ongoing investigations. And if the relationship is going to continue, it ensures that it is an equal one with no secrets and no ticking time bombs hidden in the closet.

Benefits for the addict

Some addicts see little benefit in full disclosure, as they fear the consequences, as we saw earlier in this chapter. But it is only by going through that disclosure that those fears can be truly allayed. Since there is never any guarantee that undisclosed information will not be discovered, it removes the proverbial sword of Damocles and allows energy to be channelled into recovery rather than maintaining secrecy. In addition, it reinforces accountability and genuine honesty with both self and others. Perhaps most importantly for addicts, it breaks through the shame in a powerful way by allowing the true self to be loved rather than a created self. Maintaining secrets will always damage intimacy, and for addicts to get the intimacy they so often desperately desire, full disclosure must be done.

For these benefits to be maximised, good timing is essential. A full disclosure is not advisable until some of the pain of initial disclosure has worn off and healthy coping strategies have been established for both. If there are significant additional secrets to be shared, then the disclosure process can be traumatic in itself and hence it is essential that both partners have the psychological and emotional resources to manage it. This is another reason why it is important for the process to be conducted with a trained professional who can advise on appropriate timing and ensure that both partners are able to receive the ongoing support they need.

What to disclose

In Chapter 4 we talked about how detailed information that can build visual images in the brain is unhelpful and even damaging for partners, and while this information may seem to be beneficial, it is not. As a colleague reminds clients, this is a 'therapeutic' disclosure, not a 'forensic' disclosure. Asking a partner, in an individual session, what they already know and what they feel they still need to know, normally begins the disclosure process. A therapist will then help them to think of any other questions that they want to ask. An individual session is then conducted with the addict to confirm what they've already disclosed, and go through any questions from the partner. In addition, space is provided to share any additional disclosures that need to be made. The addict will then be asked to write a disclosure letter that will include the following:

- a broad outline of all acting out behaviours and timescales;
- a broad outline of places where acting out behaviours occurred – especially if they are places known to, or special to a partner;
- any incidences of physical infidelity;
- any incidences of emotional infidelity;
- details of anyone known to the partner who was involved in acting out behaviours;
- anything that may have put a partner at risk, such as health concerns, financial and employment implications, or any illegal activities;
- any significant lies that have been told in the past to cover up behaviours.

In addition to sharing information, it is important that the letter also demonstrates remorse and empathy for the partner rather than being a catalogue of facts. In this way, partners are able to hear that the addict is taking full responsibility, not only for what happened, but also for the hurt and pain they have caused their partners.

A sample disclosure letter

Dear Sally,

This letter has taken me many hours to write and it has been one of the most painful experiences of my life. I am truly sorry for all the pain that I have caused you and I want you to know that I love you deeply and never wanted to hurt you. What follows is an account of all the ways in which I have betrayed you and put our relationship in jeopardy.

I first started viewing pornography when I was fourteen and I realise now that it had escalated out of control by the time I was in my second year of university – long before we met. I was also having sex with multiple partners, often compulsively but I didn't realise it at the time and justified to myself that it was what all young men did.

I thought all that was behind me when we met, but within the first year of our relationship I started watching pornography again. At first it was two or three times a week after you had gone to bed, but there were times when this was as much as five or six times. I used to lie to you that I was working, but I wasn't, and sometimes I didn't come to bed until the early hours of the morning. I know that this affected our sex life and I often was not available for you in the way that you deserved.

I first had an affair when you were pregnant with Archie with someone at the office. I have never felt able to tell you this before because I know what an important time that was for us and I have tainted that time forever. It was one night when we were away at a conference, and I felt huge guilt and shame. But it happened again 6 months later with the same person. After that I slept with three other women who I worked with before leaving that job.

When we moved to London I started visiting sex workers. Initially I went to massage parlours every other month but this escalated to about twice a month over the following 3 years. At the parlours I received manual stimulation and on one occasion received oral sex. In 2011 I had sex with a prostitute for the first time and that was when I realised I had a significant problem. I had sex with two other prostitutes after that until you found out last August. Since then I have not slept with anybody, but I continued viewing pornography compulsively on my work computer during office hours until March of this year. I can assure you that I have never looked at any illegal images on the computer and I have never put you at any risk of contracting a sexually transmitted infection. I have also never had sex with anyone you know or in any place that we have been to together. As far as I know, no one knows about my sexually acting out except for the people in my recovery group and the people we have told together.

Words cannot express how sorry I am for what I have done, and how much shame and guilt I feel. I know I can't expect you to forgive me or expect you to want to stay with me. But I have never stopped loving you and I promise I will do everything in my power to stop this addiction and put you and our relationship first in my life.

John

Hopefully the process of a therapeutic disclosure will leave the way open for the future, whatever that may hold, and trust can slowly be rebuilt. But sometimes a therapeutic disclosure can reveal a lot of additional painful information which may leave partners feeling back at square one again. When that occurs, partners may be thrown back into trauma and will need to go back to the strategies and self-care suggested in Chapter 4.

Managing relapse

Not everyone with an addiction has relapses, but it's not uncommon for there to be 'slips' of some kind and, regrettably, some do go through periods of relapse while on the road to recovery. Acknowledging the reality of this and how to manage it is essential to the trust-building process, and evidence shows that when people with an addiction confess their relapses, rather than waiting for them to be discovered or disclosed later, their relationships are stronger (Corley *et al.* 2012). What is more, the majority of partners had suspected a relapse, and many who weren't told went on to discover for themselves, which then had a severe detrimental effect on trust building.

It is important to understand that relapses are often part of the process of recovery, and it in no way means that someone is not committed to their relationship. There is a difference between an addict's commitment to recovery and their ability to recover, as, regrettably, a desire to stop does not automatically translate to having the tools to do so. Hence, in the early days, 'slips' or 'relapses' may be inevitable if the addiction has been severe and long-standing.

Each couple must decide for themselves what distinguishes a slip-up from a relapse, and agree what will be disclosed. It is not beneficial for partners to know every time their partner is triggered, as this can increase their feelings of insecurity, but if the trigger is not managed and leads to some kind of acting out, then some level of disclosure may be required. However, it may be agreed that switching on the computer and googling porn for a few minutes is a 'slip' and need not be disclosed, as long as the addict discusses it in therapy or in their recovery group. Similarly, walking into a massage parlour, but immediately leaving, may also not be disclosed to a partner. But if they continue to surf porn or they go through with a sexual encounter, then this almost certainly should be seen as a 'relapse' and will need to be shared.

In addition, partners can be helped to manage the possibility of relapses by considering what the consequences will be, based on what occurred. For example, you might say that if the relapse is confessed within a certain timeframe and there is demonstrable remorse, sufficient lessons learned and renewed commitment to accountability and recovery, then the relationship will most likely survive. But if the relapse continues over a period of time, such as a period of months when old behaviours have been returned to, or if there is any additional physical infidelity, then the relationship may be over.

It is, of course, impossible to know exactly how you will feel and respond if there is a relapse, and ultimately you will have to make those decisions when and if it occurs. But having some kind of plan can help to protect against the fear of relapse and strengthen personal resilience.

Evidence of recovery

Finally, partners often wonder how they can really, really know that their mates are in recovery. How can you be sure that your partner isn't just 'going through the motions' or telling you what you want to hear to make life easier for themselves? As we said earlier, it's impossible to prove that something hasn't been done, hence you will never know that they have 'not' acted out. But what you can do is see the evidence that the causes of the behaviour are being dealt with. Here is a list often measurable signs that your partner is truly in recovery:

1   Your partner is able to identify both the conscious and unconscious causes of their addiction.
2   Having identified the causes, your partner is actively working on resolving them. In other words, they're not just managing the symptoms, they're addressing the causes.
3   Your partner is 'active' in their recovery, meaning that you are able to see they are going to meetings or therapy, keeping in touch with others in recovery for support and encouragement, perhaps maintaining a regular journal or reading recovery literature.
4   Your partner is living a 'healthier' life than before. For example, they're looking after their physical health through diet and exercise and they are managing stress through relaxation and hobbies.
5   Day-to-day relationships with other people are better. That may include more contact with friends and extended family members as well as more open and engaged interaction with you and the children, if you have them.
6   Emotional connection and communication with others is also improved, including owning up to difficulties, mistakes and vulnerabilities.
7   They are more open and receptive to your emotional difficulties, mistakes and vulnerabilities and are able to let you express them appropriately without defensiveness.
8   Your partner is more assertive about their personal needs, whether physical, emotional or sexual.
9   They are proactive, not reactive to life. In other words, rather than waiting for problems to engulf them, they think ahead and take positive action to prevent difficulties arising, or take quick action to change things if they do.
10 Your partner is not perfect! If they are acting like a superhero who never has any concerns and never makes any mistakes and if they never inadvertently irritate or upset you, then something may be going on! No one is perfect and no one ever will be.

Ultimately, recovery from sex addiction is not about 'not' acting out, but about resolving the issues that led to the addiction in the first place. Addiction is a symptom of a mismanaged life. Seeing that life being managed healthily is the only true sign that someone is in recovery. And that is how couples can rebuild trust.

12 Reclaiming sex and sexuality

Sex is the furthest thing from some partners' minds and something they neither wish, nor need, to consider until many months into the recovery journey. For others, however, reclaiming sex from the shame-filled shadows of addiction helps to heal and rebuild trust and intimacy in the relationship. Others need to know if enjoying a fulfilling sex life with a partner is ever going to be possible again, before they feel able to make the decision to stay. But reclaiming a sense of positive sexuality is important for all partners, not just those who choose to stay in the couple relationship. Many partners feel that their sexuality has been robbed from them and fear they may never enjoy sex again, whether that's alone through masturbation, or with a new partner.

The way that sex and sexuality is impacted by sex addiction will depend on how they were experienced before. If sex has always been a positive experience, then it may be easier to reclaim it. But if sex has been experienced negatively, then it may seem even harder to rebuild sexual confidence and intimacy. Partners who have experienced sexual abuse in the past, whether as a child, adolescent or adult, often find it particularly difficult to find sexual confidence, especially if they have received no therapy to deal with these old trauma wounds.

In this chapter, we will explore the multiple ways that discovering sex addiction damages partners' feelings about sex and sexuality, and provide some guidance on how to develop positive sexuality again, both alone and within the current, or future, couple relationships.

Why sex matters

Being sexual is part of the nature of being human. We are all sexual beings, whether we're sexually active or not. Our sexuality includes our gender, our thoughts and our feelings about sex, whether they are positive or negative. It includes our sexual orientation, our desires, and our sexual behaviours.

Feeling comfortable and confident about our sexuality is essential for positive self-esteem, but many partners feel as if their own personal sexual identity has been contaminated by their partner's sexual addiction. Sex is also an essential part of most couple relationships. When sex is good, not only do we feel good about ourselves as individuals, but we also feel good about our relationship. A good sex life can bond couples together and help them withstand the trials and tribulations of life. Sex means different things to different people at different stages of their life. Hence the role it plays in relationships will change, depending on how long you've been together and what life stage you are at. Some partners have enjoyed a happy and fulfilling sex life with their partner right up until disclosure or discovery, for others there may always have been difficulties. Either way, sex addiction changes that and there is no going back.

Most partners find themselves wondering if they will ever enjoy their own sexuality again, and if the sex life they thought they had, was real. Many struggle with feelings of sexual inadequacy, some fear making their partner's addiction worse by having sex, or by not having sex. Many need reassurance that their partner is truly present when they're having sex, and others are desperate to get images and thoughts out of their own heads so they can be fully present themselves. Almost all partners are plagued with questions, and while the answers are unique to every individual and couple, and may take time to find, knowing that they are commonplace can provide comfort and consolation.

The questions partners ask

Will I ever want or enjoy sex again?

In the first weeks and months after disclosure or discovery, many partners experience extreme sexual aversion. For some, even the thought of being intimately touched is repulsive. Sexual feelings may completely disappear, not just desire for a partner, but desire to be sexual alone through masturbation or any kind of sexual fantasy. Many partners talk of feeling particularly sensitive and vulnerable to being looked at by others and will 'dress down' to avoid feeling sexual in any way and to avoid any unwanted or intrusive attention.

Some partners do not experience any impact on their sexual desire, but when they do have sex, they feel anxious, insecure and distracted. It may be hard to get aroused or experience orgasm or it may be difficult to enjoy particular sexual activities. For example, some who had previously been aroused by oral sex, whether giving or receiving, may find it triggers too many uncomfortable thoughts or feelings. Or certain sexual positions may now feel less intimate or too demanding or demeaning.

Sex can, and does, get better but it takes time and a committed motivation to want it for yourself. Many partners find it helpful to agree a period of sexual abstinence during which they can focus on their own feelings and needs before embarking on a sexual relationship again. There is more on abstinence and other help later in this chapter.

Will I ever be enough?

Perhaps the biggest damage to partners caused by sex addiction is the devastation it wreaks on their sexual self-confidence. Even the most stunningly beautiful sex gods and goddesses fear they will never be enough. It is essential for partners to understand that they can never compete with the sexual variety that acting out behaviours provide. People with sex addiction aren't seeking aesthetic perfection, they seek novelty, and no partner in a committed relationship can provide the endless changing landscape that addiction provides.

Some partners have gone to extreme lengths to try and become what they assume their mate wants, undergoing cosmetic surgery or learning new stimulation techniques and engaging in sexual practices that they themselves take no pleasure in. Some partners attempt to replace the porn star or the sex worker by becoming one themselves. In reality, the vast majority of people with sex addiction do not want this at all. They do not want their couple sex life to replicate their acting out behaviours, as all this does is continue their feelings of guilt and shame and blocks the ability to build the genuine, honest intimacy and connection they desperately need.

In addition to rebuilding sexual self-confidence, believing that you are enough means understanding that sex addiction is not, and never was, about sex. The behaviours satisfy the cravings of dopamine in the brain, not needs in the genitals, nor indeed desires of the heart.

Will having sex help or hinder his/her recovery?

Many partners struggle with fears that having sex, or not having sex, will impact their partner's recovery. As we discussed in the last question, ultimately sex addiction is not about sex, but nonetheless, sexual frustration can sometimes be triggering, as can certain couple sexual practices.

Coping with sexual frustration and urges will be a challenge for some sex addicts, though certainly not all. But this is a challenge that is theirs to face alone, and partners should in no way feel obligated to help them avoid addressing this piece of their recovery. No one in any sexual relationship should feel responsible for meeting all of their partner's sexual needs. Sex is always a compromise where both must learn to negotiate how their needs intertwine with their partner's to ensure that both enjoy the experience. In addiction recovery, it is essential that the addict learns to manage their desires in a healthy way. A partner who attempts to meet the addict's every sexual need could inadvertently be blocking their recovery.

If your partner is in recovery, then they will have identified any sexual behaviours that are triggering for them, that need to be avoided, at least in the early stages. For example, most people in recovery will be advised to stop watching porn, even with a partner, and this can feel penalising to partners who have previously enjoyed this as a couple. Additionally there may be some overtly erotic activities that are unhelpful, such as dressing up or engaging in role play or fantasy, that make it harder for the addict to remain fully present with a partner. Again, this can feel punitive to a non-addicted partner who has always enjoyed this.

The best way to know if having sex, or not having sex, is helping or hindering is to talk about it. Many partners who have been reluctantly having sex to 'help' their partner are both surprised, and relieved, when they discover this is not what their mate wants at all. In fact, the addict may also have been reluctantly going through with it under the false illusion that they were meeting their partner's needs.

How can I know he/she isn't fantasising about something/ someone else?

In the last chapter on rebuilding trust, we talked about how it is impossible to prove that something 'isn't happening, or hasn't happened'. Therefore, the bottom line is that you can't know that your partner isn't fantasising about someone or something else, but what you can do is become confident in the signs that they are focusing on you.

Rebuilding trust in sex is just as important as it is in every other area of the relationship, and good communication is the key. You can know that your partner is fully present with you by becoming aware of their verbal, and non-verbal, communication. If your partner talks to you during sex and listens to what you say; if they touch you in the way that you like and look at you with affection and appreciation, then they're almost certainly fully present. Eye contact is another essential sign that your partner is wholly with you. When lovers are able to maintain eye contact throughout sex, it's almost impossible to imagine being anywhere else. What is more, it promotes intimacy and connection.

Partners can increase their confidence in knowing that their partner is present by identifying both the verbal and non-verbal assurances they need, and then asking for them. In addition, it is often preferable to stick to sexual activities and positions that maximise eye contact, at least in the early stages.

How can I get the images and negative thoughts out of my head?

Many partners who feel they are recovering well in every other area of their life and their relationship, continue to struggle with negative thoughts and visual images whenever they become sexual, either alone, or with a partner. These visual images and thoughts are similar to flashbacks that trauma survivors experience and they can be extremely distressing and destructive.

Below are two techniques that can be used to overcome this, but if difficulties persist, then professional therapy can help to personalise the techniques and explore further strategies that are pertinent to individual needs and circumstances.

* **Re-orientate** – as soon as a negative thought or image occurs, remind yourself that this is a memory, this is not here and now. You can get yourself back into the present moment by using your five senses to ground you. Notice what you can see, what you can smell, what you can touch, hear and maybe taste. Communicate with your partner through talk and eye contact to help yourself become fully present in the moment.
* **Rewrite** – if there is a recurring thought or image that intrudes, then you can practise rewriting these before you get into a sexual situation. For example, negative thoughts can be rewritten into a positive, and a negative image can be replaced with a positive one. This takes practice, but in time the new positive thought will become habitual and automatically replace the negative one.

Defining 'satisfying' sexuality

The goal for all of us, whether recovering from sex addiction or not, is to enjoy 'satisfying' sexuality. In a nutshell, that means being sexually content and confident with ourselves and expressing our sexuality in a way that is fulfilling emotionally, psychologically, physically and spiritually. I include spiritually because, for many people, sex has a spiritual component, whether that is linked to a faith or a way of articulating the profound feelings of intimacy and wellbeing that sex can evoke.

Over the course of our lifetime we all pick up a host of information about what good sex means. Some of it is positive and accurate, and some is downright destructive. When we enter into a relationship, both partners bring those messages about sex with them – messages from childhood, from previous experiences, from our culture and religious faith, and also from the media. Many people have unrealistic expectations of what constitutes a satisfying sex life, and couples in recovery have the opportunity to sit down together and discuss those messages and create a definition for themselves. In short, I would define satisfying sexuality as something that meets the following core conditions:

1   In line with personal values
2   Respectful of self and others
3   Pleasurable
4   Mutually fulfilling (when partnered)
5   Not shameful
6   Confidence and esteem building

There are few rights and wrongs in sex, and each couple must decide for themselves what they are comfortable with and what will meet their personal needs. But if the core conditions above are met, then you are probably on the right track. Many couples in recovery find it helpful to put time aside to agree about what they want from a sexual relationship and to agree the vision they are heading towards. It may take time and there may be hiccups along the way, some of which may be painful, but knowing you're working together with a common goal can provide the necessary motivation and momentum required. If this feels like a difficult conversation to have alone, a couple counsellor or sex therapist can help.

Making sex better

Once you've defined what satisfying sexuality means to you, the next step is to begin to create it. For some couples, this starts by agreeing to stop having sex.

Using a period of abstinence

This may seem like an odd way to start writing about making sex better, but for some couples the best thing they can do to improve their sexual relationship is to stop for a while. Some addiction professionals will insist on a period of abstinence, often 90 days, as part of the addict's recovery. For the addict this will include masturbation as well as partnered sex. There are many reasons for this, and while some people really struggle, others welcome it as an opportunity to reset their sexual appetite and focus on recovery. Some partners also welcome the restriction, especially if they are currently sexually aversive, but others feel this is overly censorial and intrusive on their intimate couple life, and for partners who particularly enjoy sex, it also feels hugely unfair.

Whether you've jointly elected a period of abstinence, or whether it has been forced on you, there are many advantages for partners. If abstinence has not been mentioned, but you feel you would benefit, then the reasons below may help confirm that it's the right thing for you to do and help you explain to your partner. This is of course an area where 'compromise' is not possible. If one of you wants a period of abstinence, then both of you must agree to do it, and understanding the benefits can help each of you to do that graciously.

Abstinence allows time to:

- focus on rebuilding sexual self-confidence, physically and emotionally;
- work on surviving the trauma and developing stability;
- identify triggers and manage the cycle of reaction;
- develop self-care strategies;
- work on rewriting unwanted and intrusive negative thoughts and images;
- begin to rebuild trust;
- focus on developing other ways of being intimate and close;
- create confidence that your partner can cope without sex;
- develop confidence that you are appreciated and needed in non-sexual ways;
- focus on your conditions for good sex (see next section).

Getting ready for sex

Every time you have sex, whether that's after a period of abstinence or not, it is important to know that you are ready – emotionally, relationally and physically. Having sex is going to feel risky at first, and to minimise those risks it makes sense to ensure that the conditions are right. Anybody who enjoys a risky sport or hobby will tell you the importance of checking the conditions before you start. A rock climber needs to be in good physical health, have the necessary resources, trust their co-climbers, and check the weather forecast. Only when the conditions are optimum, will he or she proceed. Sex is no different, and the more you can ensure that your conditions for sex are being met, the more likely it is that you can look forward to a positive sexual encounter.

Identifying your core conditions

- **Your emotional needs** – for sex to be a positive experience, you need to be in the right frame of mind. That means choosing a time when you're not preoccupied with work or other responsibilities and when you're feeling in a good enough emotional space. It may not be realistic

---

If you've been sexually abused

If you've experienced sexual abuse in the past, then it's important to seek additional professional help and support to manage the difficult feelings that will be evoked from the past by the current situation. This will help to separate the 'then and there' from the 'here and now' and build confidence in avoiding any future sexual traumas.

---

to wait until you're completely free of any anxiety or painful emotions, but they should feel manageable.

- **Your relationship needs** – if there is a lot of tension in your relationship, then right now may not be the time to have sex. If there are problems that can be resolved, then deal with them first, if not, then ensure you are confident that the two of you are equally committed to working on them. You also need to be confident that your physical appearance or performance is not being judged and that you will receive the affirmation and assurances you need.

- **Your physical needs** – in addition to trusting that you'll get what you need in order to become aroused and stimulated, you also need to know that your physical environment is right. Many of us have some basic requirements we need in order to feel relaxed. For example, you may need to be in a warm, comfortable room, or have soft lighting and quiet. For some couples it is essential to know that they won't be disturbed or overheard. In addition, most people need to feel reasonably awake, and sober, in order to enjoy sex. They also need to feel in good health and not in too much pain or discomfort.

Saying 'no' or 'I've changed my mind'

It's much easier to feel comfortable starting something if you know you can stop if you want to. Some couples make the mistake of only initiating sex when they're 100 per cent confident that both of them are equally enthusiastic. But in the early stages of recovery, this may rarely be the case. If either of you know that you don't want sex, then it's important to feel confident in saying no, and knowing that, while your partner may be disappointed, they will be understanding and gracious about it. Furthermore, if you do decide to get intimate, it is equally important to be confident that, if one of you changes your mind, that is also going to be understood, and accepted. Having the conversation beforehand about what you will do if you decide to stop can help to avoid awkwardness, guilt and resentment.

Building sensuality

Once you have determined your conditions for sex and have met them, the next step is getting started. Being sexual is one end of a continuum, with being affectionate at the other end and sensuality somewhere in between. So the best place to begin making sex better is to get into the habit of regular physical affection. That may simply be sitting next to each other on the sofa as you watch television in the evening, getting back into the habit of kissing hello and goodbye, holding hands, having regular hugs and snuggling up in bed before going to sleep or getting up in the morning. As affection becomes more and more commonplace it's easier to slip into sensuality, turning a touch into a caress, a hug into a hold and a kiss into a smooch, touching in more intimate places and allowing increasing skin-on-skin contact. If you have plenty of free together-time, then building sensuality may be sufficient for naturally slipping into more sexual encounters, but if you lead busy lives, or have children, or both, then you may need to be more strategic.

A colleague of mine often jokes that the best sex aid a busy couple can have is a diary. Waiting for sex to happen spontaneously, when the mood is right, may be a rarity, and hence agreeing a time when you can consciously create the mood may be more pragmatic and successful. There is a common myth that sex should always be spontaneous, but planning ahead can help to build erotic anticipation as well as allowing time for any fears and anxieties to be talked through.

Trying new things

Many people recovering from sex addiction, both partners and addicts, can be fearful of being sexually adventurous and trying new things. But, for some, doing something completely new can be an effective way of reclaiming their sex life. Obviously you both need to be ready to take this step, and many couples never feel the need to, or have the desire to, but if you do, then make sure it's something you investigate together. One couple I worked with chose to explore the world of tantric sex and found a new depth of connection, intimacy and erotica that neither had ever experienced before and it revolutionised their sex life. There is much more advice on developing your sex life in the book *Erotic intelligence* (Katehakis 2010).

Overcoming sexual problems

Sexual problems can affect us all at different times of our life and at different stages of the relationship, but they are particularly common in couples recovering from sex addiction. This can be particularly frustrating for both of you and can create further feelings of insecurity. Some partners perceive their mate's lack of arousal or difficulty experiencing orgasm as a personal indictment on their lack of attractiveness or their partner's desire to be sexual. But genital functioning does not give a fair representation of what's going on inside someone's head or heart.

In this section we will look at the most common problems that can affect men and women, and some advice for overcoming them. If problems persist, or if they have been long-standing and not connected to the addiction, then further help can be found through a therapist, or further reading in the resources section at the end of this book.

Arousal difficulties

Erection problems

Erection problems are a common side-effect of heavy pornography use and it is often referred to as PIED – porn-induced erectile dysfunction. This is because constant novel sexual stimuli can increase the arousal threshold thus making it harder to be aroused just with physical contact. While common, the good news is that it normally resolves itself once porn has ceased for a period of time. Most men will experience erection problems at some stage in their life. In fact it is estimated that up to 40 per cent of men will experience problems before they are 40, and 70 per cent by the age of 70. It is important to be aware that there are some medical conditions that can cause the problem, so if in doubt, check with your doctor. But in almost all cases, psychological problems also play a part.

The most common psychological cause is anxiety, and if your partner is a male sex addict, he may feel under even more pressure than usual to ensure that sex is enjoyable for both of you. If you're a male partner, then your anxiety about being sexual may affect your ability to get aroused. The problem with anxiety is that it tends to create a self-fulfilling prophecy. The more anxious you are that you won't get an erection, the more chance there is that you won't, and hence the more anxious you become. It's a Catch-22.

The best way to cure erection problems is to understand that it's not personal, and give yourselves time. An understanding and supportive partner can help to reduce the anxiety, and the more you can stop worrying about getting an erection, the more likely it will occur.

Female arousal difficulties

In most respects, female arousal difficulties are the same as male problems with erection, but they are much less obvious and much less likely to stop you having sex. But continuing with sex if a woman is not physically aroused can be painful, and can certainly get in the way of being able to enjoy orgasm. A supportive and understanding partner is again essential, as well as learning to relax and taking time to find the best ways of being sensual and sexually stimulating.

Orgasm problems

Premature ejaculation

Most men will ejaculate faster in times of stress or after a long time without sex, both of which are common when recovering as a couple from sex addiction. It can also be a common response to feelings of guilt and shame. As with erection problems, anxiety is known to contribute to quick ejaculation, and therefore reducing anxiety is essential.

When partners can be patient and supportive, the problem should resolve itself on its own. If the problem has been long-standing, then there are additional techniques that can help, such as ensuring you focus fully on physical sensations and doing pelvic floor exercises.

Difficulty reaching orgasm (his and hers)

Struggling to reach orgasm is a common problem for both men and women recovering from sex addiction, whether you're the person with the addiction or the partner. The most common reason is stress and anxiety, but it can also be a consequence of heavy porn use. As with all sexual problems, your first line of attack is stress management and relaxation, in addition to a supportive and understanding partner. You may also find that changing stimulation techniques, and pelvic floor exercises will also help.

Mismatched sexual desire

Many couples struggle with mismatched sexual desire, and this may have been a problem long before the addiction was recognised. Each couple has to work out between them how much sex is OK in their relationship. There is no 'right' number of times to have sex. If you want sex every day and your partner wants it once a month, you're both perfectly normal. But you'll need to work together to find a compromise that both of you feel happy with.

Negotiating different sexual needs can be tricky because emotions often run high. Often one partner feels that the other is withholding and rejecting, while the other may feel that their partner's demands are unreasonable. During recovery, there can also be fears that if the higher sex drive partner is the addict, they will relapse if their needs aren't met. But conversely, if the lower sex drive partner is the addict there may be fears that they must already be acting out elsewhere.

The first step to resolving the dispute is to accept that your differences do not necessarily relate to the addiction at all and that neither of you is in the wrong. When both of you can accept each other as different, rather than wrong, you can cooperate with each other to find a solution. Both partners need to take equal responsibility for creating a relaxed and sensual environment within the home where sex is more likely to occur. To avoid any miscommunication, some couples agree 'sex-free days' where they can feel free to get close with no expectations. As discussed earlier, focusing on affection and sensuality can significantly increase the likelihood that sex will occur, as well as ensuring that basic conditions are being met.

There are many hurdles for couples recovering their individual sexuality and sex lives from sex addiction, and indeed for partners who choose to move on to new relationships. But assuming you're well on your way to resolving the emotional damage of discovery and disclosure, and you equip yourself with information about the reality of sex addiction, then sexual fulfilment can be found again. Indeed, it can be better than ever.

Conclusion

Sex addiction is a devastating condition that affects many millions of ordinary, innocent people. Not only does it wreck the lives of those who suffer with it, it also wrecks the lives of those who love them. As services in the UK and Europe slowly grow to meet the needs of sufferers, partners are often left struggling alone, feeling betrayed not only by their mates, but also by the helping professions.

Once the shock of discovery begins to wear off, most partners find themselves wrestling with overwhelming feelings of fear, rage, grief and self-doubt, but they can, and do, survive. Some choose the journey of recovery alone, others stay in their relationships and travel the road together. Either way, it is my hope that this book will provide guidance, support and encouragement for partners, and for those who want to help them on their path to a new future.

Partners of people with sex addiction are some of the bravest people I have ever met. And pulling your life back from the wreckage takes courage and compassion on a scale that I have rarely seen in any other area of my work. If this book can go some way towards helping these men and women recover their dignity, integrity and hope for the future, then it will have been a profound privilege.

References

Birchard, T. (2011) Sexual addiction and the paraphilias. *Sexual Addiction and Compulsivity: The Journal of Treatment and Prevention*, 18: 3

Black, C., Dillon, D. and Carnes, S. (2003) Disclosure to children: hearing the child's experience. *Sexual Addiction and Compulsivity: The Journal of Treatment and Prevention*, 10, 67–78

Blum, K., Braverman, E. R., Holder, J. M., Lubar, J., Monastra, V. J., Miller, D., Lubar, J., Chen, T. and Comings, D. E. (2000) Reward deficiency syndrome: a biogenetic model for the diagnosis and treatment of impulsive, addictive, and compulsive behaviors. *Journal of Psychoactive Drugs*, 32 (Suppl.), 1–112.

Carruth, B. (2006) *Psychological trauma and addiction treatment*. New York: Routledge

Corley, D. M. and Schneider, J. P. (2003) Sex addiction disclosure to children: the parents' perspective. *Sexual Addiction and Compulsivity: The Journal of Treatment and Prevention*, 10: 4, 291–324

Corley, D. M., Schneider, J. P. and Hook, J. N. (2012) Partner reactions to disclosure of relapse by self-identified sexual addicts. *Sexual Addiction and Compulsivity: The Journal of Treatment and Prevention*, 19: 4, 265–83

Dodes, L. M. (2002) *The heart of addiction: a new approach to understanding and managing alcoholism and other addictive behaviours*. New York: William Morrow

Doidge, N. (2008) *The brain that changes itself*. New York: Penguin

Duvauchelle, C., Ikegami, L. and Edward, A. C. (2000) Conditioned increases in behavioural activity and accumbens dopamine levels produced by intravenous cocaine. *Behavioural Neuroscience*, 114: 6, 1156–66

Fisher, J. (2007) *Addictions and trauma recovery*. New York: Basic Books

Flores, P. J. (2004) *Addiction as an attachment disorder*. New York: Jason Aronson

Fortuna, J. L. (2012) The obesity epidemic and food addiction: clinical similarities to drug dependence. *The Journal of Psychoactive Drugs*, 44: 1, 56–63

Fowler, J. (2006) Psychoneurobiology of co-occurring trauma and addictions. *Journal of Chemical Dependency Treatment*, 8: 2

Gilliland, R. D., South, M., Carpenter, B. and Hardy, S. (2011) The roles of shame and guilt in hypersexual behaviour. *Sexual Addiction and Compulsivity: The Journal of Treatment and Prevention*, 18, 12–29

Hall, P. (2012) *Understanding and treating sex addiction*. London: Routledge

Hall, P. (2013) A new classification model for sex addiction. *Sexual Addiction and Compulsivity: The Journal of Treatment and Prevention*, 20: 4, 279–91

Hebebrand, J., Albayrak, O., Adan, R., Antel, J., Dieguez, C., de Jong, J., Leng, G., Menzies, J., Mercer, J. G., Murphy, M., van der Plasse, G. and Dickson, S. L. (2014) 'Eating addiction', rather than 'food addiction', better captures addictive-like eating behavior. *Neuroscience and Biobehavioral Reviews*, 47, 295–306

Hentsch-Cowles, G. and Brock, L. J. (2013) A systemic review of the literature on the role of the partner of the sex addict, treatment models, and a call for research for systems theory model in treating the partner. *Sexual Addiction and Compulsivity: The Journal of Treatment and Prevention*, 20: 4, 323–35

Hilton, D. L. (2013) Pornography addiction: a supranormal stimulus considered in the context of neuroplasticity. *Socioaffective Neuroscience and Psychology*, 3: 20767

Hudson-Allez, G. (2009) *Infant searches, adult losses*. London: Karnac

Katehakis, A. (2010) *Erotic intelligence*. Deerfield Beach, FL: Health Communications

Klein, M. (2012) You're addicted to what? *The Humanist*, July/Aug

Krentzman, A. R. (2007) The evidence base for the effectiveness of alcoholics anonymous: implications for social work practice. *Journal of Social Work Practice in the Addictions*, 7: 4

Ley, D. J. (2012) *The myth of sex addiction*. Plymouth: Rowman & Littlefield

Meule, A. (2011) How prevalent is 'food addiction'? *Frontiers in Psychiatry*, 2: 61

Potter-Efron, R. (2006) Attachment, trauma and addiction, in B. Carruth (ed.), *Psychological Trauma and Addiction Treatment*. New York: Routledge

Schneider, J. P. and Levinson B. (2006) Ethical dilemmas related to disclosure issues: sex addiction therapists in the trenches. *Sexual Addiction and Compulsivity: The Journal of Treatment and Prevention*, 13: 1, 1–39

Schneider, J. P., Corley, M. D. and Irons, R. R. (1998) Surviving disclosure of infidelity: results of an international survey of 174 recovering sex addicts and partners. *Sexual Addiction and Compulsivity: The Journal of Treatment and Prevention*, 5, 189–217

Schneider, J. P., Irons, R. R. and Corley, M. D. (1999) Disclosure of extramarital sexual activities by sexually exploitative professionals and other persons with addictive or compulsive sexual disorders. *Journal of Sex Education and Therapy*, 24, 277–87

Seligman, M. (2003) *Authentic happiness: using the new positive psychology to realise your potential for lasting fulfilment*. London: Nicholas Brealey

Soloman, R. (1980) The opponent process theory of acquired motivation: the costs of pleasure and the benefits of pain. *American Psychologist*, 35: 8

Steffens, B. and Rennie, R. (2007) The traumatic nature of disclosure for wives of sexual addicts. *Sexual Addiction and Compulsivity: The Journal of Treatment and Prevention*, 13, 247–67

Steffens, B. and Means, M. (2009) *Your sexually addicted spouse.* Far Hills, NJ: New Horizon Press

Tripodi, C. (2006) Long term treatment of partners of sex addicts: a multi-phase approach. *Sexual Addiction and Compulsivity: The Journal of Treatment and Prevention*, 13: 2–3, 269–88

Turnbull, G. (2011) *Trauma. From Lockerbie to 7/7: how trauma affects our minds and how we fight back.* London: Corgi Books

Voon, V., Mole, T. B., Banca, P., Porter, L., Morris, L., Mitchell, S., Lapa, T. R., Karr, J., Harrison, N. A., Potenza, M. N. and Irvine, M. (2014). Neural correlates of sexual cue reactivity in individuals with and without compulsive sexual behaviours. *PLoS ONE*, 9: 7

Recommended reading and resources

The following books are for professionals as well as for general readers. Some I have personally read and would recommend, others have been found useful by others. My advice would be to look them up on Amazon and decide from there that would best suit your personal situation and circumstances.

Books

About sex addiction

Always turned on: sex addiction in the digital age, Robert Weiss and Jennifer Schneider (Gentle Path Press)
CBT for Compulsive Sexual Behaviour: a guide for professionals, Thaddeus Birchard (Routledge)
Closer together, further apart: the effect of technology and the internet on parenting, work and relationships, Robert Weiss and Jennifer Schneider (Gentle Path Press)
Cruise control: understanding sex addiction in gay men, Robert Weiss (Alyson Publications)
Don't call it love: recovery from sexual addiction, Patrick Carnes (Bantam, New York)
Erotic intelligence: igniting hot, healthy sex while in recovery from sex addiction, Alexandra Katehakis (Health Communications)
In the shadows of the net: breaking free from compulsive online sexual behaviour, Patrick Carnes, David Delmonico and Elizabeth Griffin (Hazelden)
Making advances: a comprehensive guide for treating female sex and love addicts, edited by Marnie Ferree (CreateSpace)
Out of the shadows: understanding sex addiction, Patrick Carnes (Hazelden)
The porn trap: the essential guide to overcoming problems caused by pornography, Wendy Maltz and Larry Maltz (Harper)
Understanding and treating sex addiction: a comprehensive guide for people who struggle with sex addiction and those who want to help them, Paula Hall (Routledge)

Untangling the web: sex, porn and fantasy obsession in the internet age, Robert Weiss and Jennifer Schneider (Alyson Books)

For partners

Codependent no more: how to stop controlling others and start caring for yourself, Melody Beattie (Hazelden)
Disclosing secrets: an addicts guide for when, to whom, and how much to reveal, Deborah Corley and Jennifer Schneider (Recovery Resources Press)
Facing co-dependence: what it is, where it comes from, how it sabotages our lives, Pia Mellody (HarperOne)
Mending a shattered heart: a guide for partners of sex addicts, edited by Stefanie Carnes (Gentle Path Press)
Surviving disclosure: a partner's guide for healing the betrayal of intimate trust, Jennifer Schneider and Deborah Corley (Recovery Resources Press)
Your sexually addicted spouse: how partners can cope and heal, Barbara Steffens and Martha Means (New Horizon Press)

About addiction

Addiction as an attachment disorder, Philip J. Flores (Aronson)
Learning the language of addiction counseling, Geri Miller (Wiley)
Psychological trauma and addiction treatment, edited by Bruce Carruth (Routledge)
The fix, Damien Thompson (Collins)
Theory of addiction, Robert West (Wiley-Blackwell)

About general psychology and self-help

Attached: the new science of adult attachment and how it can help you find and keep love, Amir Levine and Rachel Heller (Tarcher)
Authentic happiness, Martin Seligman (Nicholas Brealey)
Boosting self esteem for dummies, Rhena Branch and Rob Willson (Wiley)
Emotional intelligence: why it can matter more than IQ, Daniel Goleman (Bloomsbury)
Managing anger: simple steps for dealing with frustration and threat, Gael Lindenfield (Thorsons)
People skills: how to assert yourself, listen to others and resolve conflicts, Robert Bolton (Touchstone)
The body remembers: a psychophysiology of trauma and trauma treatment, Babette Rothschild (Norton)
The chimp paradox: the mind management programme, Steve Peters (Vermillion)
The mindful brain, Daniel Siegel (Norton)
Wherever you go, there you are, Jon Kabat-Zinn (Hearst Publications)

About relationships and sexuality

Better than ever: love and sex at mid life, Bernie Zilbergeld (Crown House Publishing)

Coping with erectile dysfunction: how to regain confidence and enjoy great sex, Michael Metz (New Harbinger)

Coping with premature ejaculation: how to overcome PE, Michael Metz (New Harbinger)

Couples and sex: an Introduction to relationship dynamics and psychosexual concepts, Carol Martin-Sperry (Routledge)

Erotic intelligence: igniting hot, healthy sex while in recovery from sex addiction, Alexandra Katehakis (Health Communications Inc)

Improving your relationship for dummies, Paula Hall (Wiley Press)

I'm OK, you're OK, Thomas Harris (Arrow)

Help your children cope with your divorce, Paula Hall (Vermillion)

How to have a healthy divorce, Paula Hall (Vermillion)

Loving yourself, loving another: the importance of self esteem for successful relationships, Julia Cole (Vermillion)

Recovering intimacy in love relationships: a clinicians guide, Jon Carlson and Len Sperry (Routledge)

Rekindling desire: a step-by-step program to help low sex and no-sex marriages, Barry and Emily McCarthy (Brunner-Routledge)

Rewriting the rules: a new guide to love, sex and relationships, Meg Barker (Routledge)

Stop arguing, start talking: the 10 point plan for couples in conflict, Susan Quilliam (Vermillion)

The guide to getting it on, Paul Joannides (Goofy Foot Press)

Women without sex: the truth about female sexual problems, Catherine Kalamis (Self Help Direct Publishing)

Psychotherapy, counselling and treatment services

For sex addiction

ATSAC (Association for the Treatment of Sexual Addiction and Compulsivity) – www.ATSAC.co.uk. The UK's professional association for sex addiction professionals provides a register of therapists specialising in sex addiction treatment and training for professionals

ISAT (Institute for Sex Addiction Training) – www.instituteforsexaddiction training.co.uk. A UK-based training organisation specialising in sex addiction training for professionals

Kick Start Recovery Programme – www.sexaddictionhelp.co.uk. A free online resource created by Paula Hall to help individuals struggling with sex and porn addiction

Paula Hall – www.paulahall.co.uk. Information and UK-wide support services for individuals struggling with sex and porn addiction

Recovery Nation – www.recoverynation.com. A recovery website that provides online recovery tools for sex addicts, partners and couples along with expert coaching and community support

SAA (Sex Addicts Anonymous) – www.saa-recovery.org.uk. Peer support groups for sex addicts following the 12-step principles. Meetings around the UK

SLAA (Sex and Love Addicts Anonymous) – www.slaauk.org. Peer support groups for sex addicts following the 12-step principles. Meetings around the UK

The Hall Recovery Course – www.thehallrecoverycourse.co.uk. Weekly, intensive and residential recovery courses for people struggling with sex and porn addiction

The Priory Group – www.priorygroup.com. A group of multi-disciplinary treatment centres around the UK that provide residential and out-patient treatment for sex addiction

Your Brain On Porn website – www.yourbrainonporn.com. A science-based website that provides information about the impact of pornography and recovery advice for those whose porn use is a problem

For partners

COSA – www.cosa-recovery.org. A 12-step recovery programme for male and female partners whose lives have been affected by sex addiction

Paula Hall – www.paulahall.co.uk. Information and nationwide support services for partners of people with sex and porn addiction

POSARC – www.posarc.com. An online information resource for partners of sex addicts

For individual and relationship issues

College of Sexual and Relationship Therapy – www.cosrt.org.uk. Provides information on sexual problems and a register of private therapists who specialise in relationship and sexual problems

Pink Therapy – www.pinktherapy.com. The UK's largest independent therapy organisation working with gender and sexual minority clients

Relate – www.relate.org.uk. The UK's largest counselling service for couples and individuals with sexual or relationship difficulties. Also provides services for young people and families

Relationships Scotland – www.relationships-scotland.org.uk. Provides counselling for relationship and sexual problems to individuals and couples throughout Scotland

The British Association of Counselling and Psychotherapy – www.bacp.co.uk. Provides a register of private counsellors and psychotherapists who can work with a wide range of problems

Index

Note: page numbers in *italic* type refer to Figures; those in **bold** type refer to Tables.

12-step groups 7, 94, 131

absence (of parent), and attachment-induced addiction 22
abstinence, sexual 145, 148–9
abuse: and attachment-induced addiction 22; domestic abuse 113; and trauma-induced addiction 21
accountability 103, 132–4
accountability contracts 99, 132–4, 134–5
acting out phase of sex addiction 24, *24*, 27
addict/co-dependent roles in couple relationship 122
addiction: cycle of 23–5, *24*; definition of 8; and early exposure 16; neurochemistry of 6, 8, 15–16; *see also* sex addiction
adolescence: and lying 130; and opportunity-induced addiction 19, 20
adrenalin 15
affairs, and sex addiction 29–30
affirmations 54, 65, 81–2
American Association for Addiction Medicine (ASAM) 8
amygdala 20
anger 37, 47–9, 69–70

anxiety 52–4, 70; and erectile dysfunction 152; and premature ejaculation 153
arousal difficulties 152–3
ASAM (American Association for Addiction Medicine) 8
assault, and trauma-induced addiction 21
ATSAC (Association for the Treatment of Sexual Addiction and Compulsivity) 25, 94
attachment-induced addiction 18, *18*, 21–3; and unconscious couple collusions 121
attachment, healthy 22
autonomy, in relationships 130

'behavioural' addictions 7–8
bereavement 56; and trauma-induced addiction 21
betrayal 29, 103
blame (cognitive distortions) 67
boundaries, and co-dependency 100, 103–4
brain: and dopamine 6, 10, 15, 23, 145; and food addiction 8; hypersensitivity to arousal 23; neurochemistry of addiction 6, 8, 15–16
BREATHE strategy 64–5

brother/sister roles in couple
relationship 122

Carnes, Patrick 21, 32
checking 70, 98–9
child protection procedures 40
children: needs of 110, 114–16; risk of
sex addicts to 33, 40; telling about
sex addiction 57, 114, 126
co-dependency 31–2, 95–6; addict/co-
dependent roles in couple
relationship 122; avoidance of
103–4; definition of 96–8;
identification of 98–103;
overcoming 104–5
cognitive distortions 66–8
Coleman, Eli 32
Commit to recovery (UR-CURED
process) 25, 26
conclusions, jumping to (cognitive
distortions) 66
contribution, to society 88
control 92, 101
COSA 94
counselling 93–4
couple relationship: communication in
123–5; impact of sex addiction on
117–27; impact on sexual
relationship 126–7; length and life
stage of 120; as part of a balanced
lifestyle 86; quality of 120–1;
survival of 51, 57, 107–16;
unconscious couple collusions
121–2; *see also* sexual
relationship of couple
courage 79
cover-ups 99
cycle of reaction 59, **60**, 105;
breaking 73; dormant phase
59–63, *60*; preparation phase
60, 65–8; reactive emotions and
behaviours phase *60*, 69–71;
reconstitution phase *60*, *72–3*;
regret phase *60*, 71–2; trigger
phase *60*, 63–5
cycle of sex addiction 23–5, *24*

defensiveness 119
deferred gratification 16
denial 67, 112, 119
depression 71
despair 50–1, 70–1, 119
detective breakthrough disclosure **36**,
38
Develop a healthy life (UR-CURED
process) 25, 27
Diagnostic and Statistics Manual
(DSM) 8
diet 80
disclosure 110; discovery/disclosure
process **36**, 36–8, 41, 43–58;
inappropriate 69–70; therapeutic
disclosure 135–8
disconnection 46–7
disgust 55
dissociation 45, 46–7
distraction 55
domestic abuse 113
dopamine 6, 10, 15, 23, 145
dormant phase: of cycle of reaction
59–63, *60*, 72; of sex addiction 24,
24, 27
drip, drip, drip disclosure/exposure **36**,
37
DSM (Diagnostic and Statistics
Manual) 8

early warning systems, for anger
management 49
emotional contact 104
emotional reasoning (cognitive
distortions) 66
emotions, difficult: and opportunity-
induced addiction 19; self-soothing
behaviours 20
empathy 132
endorphins 15
erectile dysfunction 152
escalation (addiction) 15–16
Establish relapse prevention strategies
(UR-CURED process) 25, 27
excuses 99
exercise 49, 80

Face the future (SURF process) 41,
85–94, 105
family 86–7, 104
fear 52–4, 70
fetish behaviours 20
financial issues 104, 110
food addiction, and the brain 8
forgiveness 91–2, 113
friendship 80–1, 86, 104
fun 81, 87

grief 50–1, 70–1
grounding exercises 46–7
group work: and honesty 131;
for partners of sex addicts
54–5, 87, 94
guilt 26

Hall Recovery Courses for Partners 94
healthy life, development of 27, 79–80
helplessness (cognitive distortions) 67
hindsight 34
home environment 104
honesty 131; *see also* lying; trust
hook-up sites 9
humanity 79
hypervigilance 70, 98–9
hypo-arousal 20

idol/worshipper roles in couple
relationship 122
impulse control 16
inadequate parenting, and attachment-
induced addiction 22–3
independence 102
individual therapy 94, 131
infidelity, and sex addiction 29–30
information-seeking/investigation
52–3, 57–8, 67–8
internet: impact on brain chemistry
16; online support groups 94; and
sex/porn addiction 10–11, 19
intimacy 32–3

justice 79, 92
justification (cognitive distortions) 66

knowledge 78

life wheel 89, *89*
lifeline exercise 61–3
lifestyle, balanced 86–91, *89*
loneliness, in adolescence 20
lying 129–30; *see also* honesty; trust

magnification (cognitive distortions)
66
masturbation 20, 144
Means, Marsha 83
medical help, and shock 46
mindfulness 53, 55
minimisation (cognitive distortions) 66
moral failure, sex addiction as 6–7
motivation, opponent-process theory
of 20

negligence, and attachment-induced
addiction 22
neurochemistry of addiction 6, 8, 15–16
normalisation (cognitive distortions)
67

OATS model (opportunity-,
attachment- and trauma-induced
sex addiction) 17–23, *18*
online support groups 94
opponent-process theory of acquired
motivation 20
opportunity-induced addiction *18*,
18–20
orgasm problems 153
overcompensation 99–100
overreaction 35

panic attacks 70
paraphilias 20
parent/child roles in couple
relationship 121
parenting, and attachment-induced
addiction 22–3
partners of sex addicts: anger 37,
47–9, 69–70; co-dependency 31–2,
95–105; cognitive distortions 66–8;

common assumptions and
misunderstandings 29–35;
communication needs 123; cycle of
reaction 41, 59–73, *60*, 105;
discovery/disclosure process **36**,
36–8, 41, 43–58; disgust 55; facing
the future 41, 85–94, 105; fear and
anxiety 52–4, 70; forgiveness
91–2, 113; grief and despair 50–1,
70–1; help available to 93–4;
questions about sexual relationship
144–7; reactions of 118; relief 56;
self-blame 47; self-harm 47, 70,
100; self-identity and self-esteem
75–83, *76*, *78*, 105; shame 38, 40,
54–5; shock **36**, 36–7, 43, 45–7,
105; suicidal feelings 47, 50;
survival of couple relationship 51,
57, 107, 109–16; urgent questions
56–8; *see also* couple relationship
Partners of Sex Addicts Resource
Center (PoSARC) 94
peace keeping behaviour 99
people pleasing behaviour 99
perfectionism 101
personal growth 88
physical assault 69
physical contact 104
physical health 79–80
PIED (porn-induced erectile
dysfunction) 152
pillars 54, 79, 82–3
porn addiction 5, 9, 40; and the brain
8; and the internet 10–11, 19; and
intimacy 32
porn-induced erectile dysfunction
(PIED) 152
PoSARC (Partners of Sex Addicts
Resource Center) 94
positive self-talk 54, 65, 81–2
post-traumatic stress disorder (PTSD)
43
premature ejaculation 153
preparation phase: of cycle of reaction
60, 65–8; of sex addiction 24, *24*,
27

'process' addictions 7–8
PTSD (post-traumatic stress disorder)
43

rationalisations (cognitive distortions)
66
re-orientation 147
reactive emotions and behaviours
phase of cycle of reaction *60*,
69–71
reconstitution phase: of cycle of
reaction *60*, *72–3*; of sex addiction
24, 25, 27
recovery 27–8, 31, 111; commitment
to 110; and the couple's sexual
relationship 145–6; evidence of
140–1
recreation 81, 87
Reduce shame (UR-CURED process)
25, 26
regret phase: of cycle of reaction *60*,
71–2; of sex addiction *24*, 25, 27
relapse prevention 27
relapse, management of 139
Relate 10, 94
relationship *see* couple relationship
relaxation 49, 87
relief 56
Repairing self-identity/self-esteem
(SURF process) 41, 75–83, *76*, *78*,
105
Resolve underlying issues
(UR-CURED process) 25, 27
responsibility 111, 112
rewriting 147
risk 134–5

safety 92
Sanders, Deirdre 10
scab picking 68
secrecy, and opportunity-induced
addiction 19–20
self-blame 47
self-care 83
self-control, and opportunity-induced
addiction 19

self-esteem, repairing of 77–83, *78*
self-harm 47, 70, 100
self-identity, repairing of 75–7, *76*, 79
Seligman, Martin 78
sensuality 151
sex: and the brain 8, 10; importance of 143–4; improving 148–51
sex addiction: advantages to label of 13; assessment questions 11–12; classifications of (OATS model) 17–23, *18*; common assumptions and misunderstandings 29–35; common objections to 6–10; evidence for 10–11; existence of 5–13, **39**; impact on couple relationship 117–27; and intimacy 32–3; range of behaviours 9–10; recovery from 27–8, 110, 140–1, 145–6; risk to children 33; six-phase cycle of 23–5, *24*, 26–7; start of 16–17, 19; survival of couple relationship 51, 57, 107, 109–16; treatment of 25–7; understanding 15–28; *see also* addiction
sex addicts: communication needs 123, 125; reactions of 118–19; *see also* couple relationship
sex education, and opportunity-induced addiction 19, 20
sexual abstinence 145, 148–9
sexual abuse 150
sexual health fears 53
sexual offending 33
sexual problems 151–4
sexual relationship of couple: 'satisfying' sexuality 147–8; impact on 126–7; importance of 143–4; improving 148–51; overcoming sexual problems 151–4; partners' questions 144–7; *see also* couple relationship
shame 119; and opportunity-induced addiction 19; partners of sex addicts 38, 40, 54–5; Reduce shame (UR-CURED process) 25, 26

shock: of the discovery/disclosure process **36**, 36–7, 43, 45–7; medical help 46; physical symptoms of 45; survival strategies 46–7; trauma-induced addiction 21
'signature strengths' 78
six-phase cycle of sex addiction 23–5, *24*, 26–7
sledgehammer blow **36**, 36–7
sleep 80
SMART (specific, measurable, achievable, relevant and time-related) goals 89–91
social stigma 38, 40, 114
socialising, and partners of sex addicts 51, 80–1
Steffens, Barbara 83
STIs (sexually transmitted infections) 53
suicidal feelings, of partners of sex addicts 47, 50
SURF process 41, 105; Face the future 41, 85–94; Repairing self-identity/self-esteem 41, 75–83, *76*, *78*; Survive the trauma of discovery 41, 43–58; Understand cycle of reaction 41, 59–73, *60*
survival, of couple relationship 51, 57, 107; children's needs 114–16; postponing decision-making about 109–10; reasons to separate 110–12; reasons to stay 110–12
Survive the trauma of discovery (SURF process) 41, 43–58, 105

temperance 79
therapeutic disclosure 135–8
therapy: and honesty 131; for partners of sex addicts 93–4
Three Cs 83, 105
tolerance (addiction) 15–16
transcendence 79
trauma: and the discovery/disclosure process **36**, 36–7, 38; Survive the trauma of discovery (SURF

process) 41, 43–58; symptoms of
97–8
trauma-induced addiction 18, *18*,
20–1
trial separation 112
trigger phase: of cycle of reaction *60*,
63–5; of sex addiction 24, *24*, 27
trust 112, 129–30; couple's sexual
relationship 146; essential
ingredients of 130–5; evidence of
recovery 140–1; managing relapse
139; therapeutic disclosure 135–8;
see also honesty; lying

Understand cycle of addiction
(UR-CURED process) 25, 26–7
Understand cycle of reaction (SURF
process) 41, 59–73, *60*, 105

Understand sex addiction
(UR-CURED process) 26–7
uniqueness (cognitive distortions) 66
UR-CURED process 25–7

values 77, 113
'ventilation sessions' 123–5
verbal attacks 69
victim stance (cognitive distortions) 66
victim/rescuer roles in couple
relationship 122
violence 113

wisdom 78
withdrawal 70–1
work, as part of a balanced lifestyle
87–8
woundedness 119